Breakfast is Served
in the
St. Croix Valley

A BED AND BREAKFAST GUIDE

BY DIANE MEHRA

Photographs by Debra Chial, Diane Mehra,
and Mary Perkins

Edited by Sara Saetre

COVER DESIGN BY JOAN GORDON

IM-PRESS ENTERPRISES
Stillwater, Minnesota

Front Cover photographs:
Mrs. LaFuegy's Room from the Wm. Sauntry Mansion, Stillwater, MN.
Taken by Mary Perkins
Breakfast at the Elephant Walk, A Bed & Breakfast, Stillwater, MN.
Taken by Debra Chial.

Back cover:
The Cave Suite at The Old Jail Company, Taylors Falls, MN.
Taken by Debra Chial.

Credited photographs are copyright by the photographers
Photos provided by Deb Chial Photography and Mary Perkins - Click.

Published by Im-Press Enterprises
P.O. Box 704
Stillwater, MN 55082

Printed in USA by Viking Press, Eden Prarie, MN

Library of Congress Catalog Card Number: 93-61342
ISBN 0-9637143-0-9

Breakfast is Served in the St. Croix Valley

A Bed & Breakfast Guide

Front entrance to the James A Mulvey Residence Inn, Stillwater.

Photo by Deb Chial.

Acknowledgements

One does not accomplish a task such as this without the encouragement and assistance of many people. Primarily I would like to extend my gratitude to Sara Saetre, my editor, whom I approached with the premise of doing this book over a year ago. She has been an invaluable aid; offering encouragement and keen advice. Mr. Charles Claude, of SCORE, has also served as an advisor on this project and I have gained from this association — my thanks to him. Without the talents of photographers, Deb Chial and Mary Perkins and cover designer Joan Gordon this book would not have been a visual showcase. For the 'keepers of the inns' I have much appreciation. Their enthusiasm and cooperation made my task more enjoyable. To Paula Tierney of Word Processing & More and Sue Kusilek, I am indebted for their perseverance in bringing this book to print. Much of the information contained in the historical outlines and points of interest came from the area's chambers of commerce or local historical society. I feel that this information makes the book more valuable and extend thanks to these services for their assistance.

A large part of the credit in bringing this book to completion is due my family. My husband Rahul and children Kiran and Anjali have been supportive and patient. And to a very special person, Manuela Steffen, who helped look after my family in a loving and caring manner for the past year, I say, "Danke Viel Mals".

CONTENTS

Map vii
How To Use This Guide viii
Foreword ix

INTRODUCTION 1

SECTION I
The St. Croix Valley - An Overview 2

SECTION II
Lower St. Croix Valley

  A.   Historical Outlines and Points of Interest 6

  B.   Bed & Breakfast Guide
     A Country Rose B & B, Hastings, MN. 10
     Rosewood Inn, Hastings, MN. 10
     Thorwood Inn, Hastings, MN. 12
     The Arbor Room, Prescott, WI. 13
     The Oak Street Inn, Prescott, WI 14
     The Inn on the Hill, Prescott, WI 15
     Afton Country B & B, Afton, MN 16
     The Afton House Inn, Afton, MN. 17
     River Elms Carriage House, Lakeland, MN. 18
     The Knollwood House, River Falls, WI 19
     The Trillium Woods B & B, River Falls, WI.......... 20
     The Bluebird Cottage B & B, Hudson, WI 21
     The Boyden House, Hudson, WI 22
     The Grapevine Inn, Hudson, WI 23
     The Jefferson–Day House, Hudson, WI 24
     The 1884 Phipps Inn, Hudson, WI.................... 26
     The Stageline Inn, Hudson, WI 27
     Summit Farm B & B, Hammond, WI 28
     The Kaleidoscope Inn, Baldwin, WI 29

  C.   Lower St. Croix Valley B & B Photo Guide 31

SECTION III
Central St. Croix Valley

  A.   Historical Outlines and Points of Interest 47

B. Bed & Breakfast Guide
   Cover Park Manor, Oak Park Hts, MN 50
   The Ann Bean House, Stillwater, MN 50
   Battle Hollow B & B, Stillwater, MN 52
   Brunswick Inn, Stillwater, MN 53
   The Elephant Walk B & B, Stillwater, MN 54
   The Heirloom Inn, Stillwater, MN....................................55
   The James A. Mulvey Residence Inn, Stillwater, MN. 56
   The Laurel Street Inn, Stillwater, MN 57
   The Lowell Inn, Stillwater, MN....................................59
   The Outing Lodge at Pine Point, Stillwater, MN 60
   Rivertown Inn, Stillwater, MN 62
   The Wm. Sauntry Mansion, Stillwater, MN. 63
   Shady Ridge Farm B & B, Houlton, WI 64
   The Asa Parker House, Marine on Croix, MN 65
   Pleasant Lake B & B, Osceola, WI 66
   St. Croix River Inn, Osceola, WI 67

C. Central St. Croix Valley B & B Photo Guide 71

SECTION IV
  Upper St. Croix Valley

A. Historical Outlines and Points of Interest 87

B. Bed & Breakfast Guide
   Amberwood B & B, St. Croix Falls, WI 92
   The Country Bed and Breakfast, Shafer, MN 93
   The Old Franconia Hotel B & B, Shafer, MN 94
   The Cottage, Taylors Falls, MN. 95
   The McLane House, Taylors Falls, MN 96
   The Old Jail Company, Taylors Falls, MN 97
   The Boathouse, Lindstrom, MN. 98
   The Red Pine B & B, N. Branch, MN 99
   Tree Top Hts. B & B, Balsam Lake, WI............................100
   Gandy Dancer B & B, Frederic, WI............................101
   Seven Pines Lodge, Lewis, WI 102
   Forgotten Tymes B & B, Siren, WI....................................103
   Aunt Martha's Guest House , Spooner, WI............................104
   Wildflower, Danbury, WI 105
   Dakota Lodge, Hinckley, MN 106
   Victorian Rose, Finlayson, MN 107
   The Stout Trout B & B, Springbrook, WI 108

C. Upper St. Croix Valley B & B Photo Guide 111

SECTION V
  Information Guide 124

A. Area Chambers of Commerce & Tourism offices
B. Fine Dining, Antique and Specialty Shops, Special Attractions,&
   Special Events

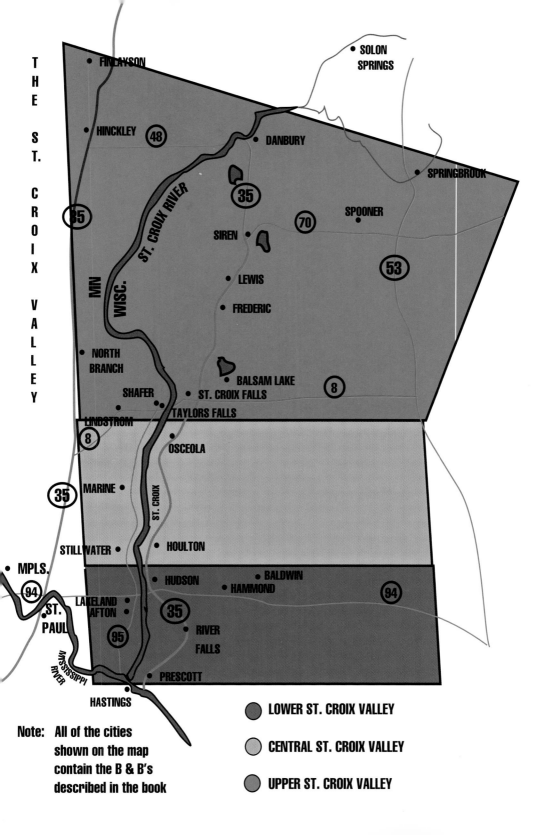

THE ST. CROIX VALLEY

FINLAYSON

SOLON SPRINGS

HINCKLEY (48)

DANBURY

SPRINGBROOK

ST. CROIX RIVER

(35)

(35)

SPOONER

(70)

SIREN

(53)

MN

WISC.

LEWIS

FREDERIC

NORTH BRANCH

SHAFER

BALSAM LAKE

ST. CROIX FALLS

(8)

TAYLORS FALLS

LINDSTROM

(8)

OSCEOLA

MARINE

(35)

ST. CROIX

STILLWATER

HOULTON

MPLS.

(94)

BALDWIN

HUDSON

HAMMOND

(94)

LAKELAND

ST. PAUL

AFTON

(35)

RIVER FALLS

(95)

MISSISSIPPI RIVER

PRESCOTT

HASTINGS

Note: All of the cities shown on the map contain the B & B's described in the book

🔴 LOWER ST. CROIX VALLEY

🟡 CENTRAL ST. CROIX VALLEY

🔵 UPPER ST. CROIX VALLEY

How to Use This Guide

All of the B & Bs described here are inspected and licensed by either the states of Minnesota or Wisconsin. Breakfast, either continental style or full fare with hot entrées are included in the prices. In most cases, **reservations are made with advance payment**. Prices and policies are current for the year of 1993.

I have organized this book so that entries are listed geographically by city within each of the three regions of the valley: Lower St. Croix Valley, Central St. Croix Valley, and Upper St. Croix Valley regions. Refer to the map in the beginning of this book to locate cities.

To make this guide more useful, I have included an overview of the St. Croix River Valley, and each section begins with historical outlines and points of interest in the area described followed by descriptions of the B & Bs. Photos are organized for the B & Bs described. There is a section listing area chambers of commerce, departments of tourism, as well as a listing of special events occurring throughout the year. For your convenience I have also included a listing of area fine dining, specialty shops and special attractions.

To keep this guidebook up-to-date an invitation is extended to users of this guide to inquire about current prices and policies of the B & Bs for the coming years of 1994 and 1995. Send a stamped, self-addressed envelope to the address below and state you want an up-to-date listing of any price or policy change of the B & Bs included in this guide during this time period.

IM-PRESS ENTERPRISES
Diane Mehra
P O Box 704
Stillwater, MN. 55042

For copies of this guide, send $14.95
plus $1.50 for shipping to the above address.
(Minnesota residents add sales tax.)

Copies of this book also available in bookstores and many of the B&Bs

FOREWORD

I trust a good deal to common fame, as we all must. If a man has good corn, or wood, or boards, and pigs to sell, or can make better chairs or knives, crucibles or church organs than anybody else, you will find a broad, hard beaten road to his house, though it be in the woods.

Ralph Waldo Emerson, Journals.

There are many broad hard beaten roads in the St. Croix River Valley, as evidenced in this delicious journey. Diane Mehra has traveled them all. Her spirit of adventure, her background in history and her love of the valley are obvious.

The industry of Bed and Breakfast Innkeeping in the area began in the early 1980s. Keepers of the Small Inn (as we like to call ourselves) would get together and share potluck and restoration stories. When there were just a few inns, we would take turns hostessing and had the opportunity to learn about each other's offerings. This gave us the opportunity to share with our guests information about our area and other inns too. The area now boasts over fifty inns, some as close together as a few houses between and some as far apart as twenty miles.

Look back at how this area was settled and realize the importance of this great river and contemplate how lucky we are to have the advantages of this legacy. Listen to the stories to be told in these rivertowns by shopkeepers and innkeepers. Listen to the sharing here in this guide encouraging this journey. Know and learn and love that you are welcomed here in the valley. Enjoy the broad, hard beaten roads with Diane Mehra as your compass.

Pam Thorsen, Keeper of the Thorwood and Rosewood Inns

INTRODUCTION

I became aware that the number of B & Bs were increasing at such a fast rate in my hometown of Stillwater, Minnesota, that I could hardly keep pace with their presence. These old neglected homes suddenly seemed to announce their "renewal" and became so engaging from the curbside, as if beckoning, "Come in, you're welcome." Often I leapt from my car with excitement, hoping that the owner was at home and would be gracious enough to show me what I had expected from the outside. Without fail I was fortunate to find a most charming and enthusiastic innkeeper who very promptly invited me to enter and proudly gave me a tour, adding the details of all their undertakings and history of the home.

Soon I found that Hudson, a neighboring town across the St. Croix River on the Wisconsin side, had developed three B & Bs in old historic homes. When I set out to explore further up and down the river, I found this was not an isolated occurrence; many communities in the river valley had experienced such a blossoming of B & Bs.

In fact, I found fifty of these retreats. More than half had been established in the past two-and-a-half years. Now, you might wonder why I took such an avid interest in this industry. In the past years I have travelled over the USA, Canada, Europe, and Asia, enjoying the pleasure of bed and breakfast accommodations, and coming away with the fondest memories not only of places but also of people.

But I was always glad to return home. Having moved to the St. Croix Valley a decade ago from New York City, I believe that I have found my own special place. My delight in the natural beauty of the valley in every season, combined with the character of its citizens and the attractiveness of its old rivertowns, has been the impetus for this book. It is my belief that the resplendence of the St. Croix Valley and the emergence of outstanding bed and breakfasts here will gratify any visitor as well.

I have visited each of these fifty historic homes, inns, lodges, and special places. No establishment has paid any gratuity or fee to be included in this book. The homes each have their own singular delight, and delight they do. For today bed and breakfasts don't just provide a traveler's rest, but also pamper, nurture, entertain, and charm their guests. Customer-focused, quality service is not a watchword but a fact.

The bed and breakfasts here are presented in descriptive text and showcased in full-color photographs so that readers can gain a real sense of the wealth of experiences the St. Croix Valley has to offer.

Section I. THE ST. CROIX VALLEY

The River

Before the World Champion Minnesota Twins, Super Bowl XXVII, and the Mall of America, one of Minnesota's most appreciated attractions has been the St. Croix Valley. The St. Croix is one of the most beautiful rivers in the Midwest. Many hundreds of thousands of years ago, masses of melted ice flooded the land of this region and carved out this dramatically scenic and beautiful valley. On the geologic clock, little has changed since that time and much of the riverway remains the same.

Forming much of the border of eastern Minnesota and northwestern Wisconsin, the pristine waters of the St. Croix River have their source at what is called upper Lake St. Croix, just east of the village of Solon Springs, Wisconsin. From there the river takes a journey southward for some 165 miles to the place called Point Douglas, near Prescott, Wisconsin. Here it empties itself into the more renowned, mightier "Father of Waters," the Mississippi. The area drained by this river, the St. Croix Valley, is claimed by Wisconsin on its eastern banks and Minnesota on its western banks.

The upper river is more narrow and wild and fast flowing, containing sections of rapids challenging for any canoeist. As the river makes its course southward from Highway 70 to the city of St. Croix Falls, it broadens some and becomes more slow moving. Below the Nevers Dam at Taylors Falls, the river banks change and are characterized by high bluffs of basaltic rock commonly referred to as The Dalles of the St. Croix. The waters are slow moving and excellent for small boats and canoeists. At just below Stillwater, the river's waters broaden to their widest and form what is called Lake St. Croix. In this section of the river the waters are deeper, with vistas of long, broad, rolling hills. You'll find pleasure boating, water skiing, and sailing on the river in warm weather, and ice fishing in winter. The river then winds south for another thirty miles until it reaches Point Douglas, where it unites with the Mississippi.

In 1968 the National Wild and Scenic Rivers Act declared the St. Croix River a National and Scenic Riverway to be protected as an area of natural and scenic value and for outdoor recreation.

Today the river offers a common experience of unpolluted waters, and richness in wildlife and flora, to both the citizens of Minnesota and Wisconsin as well as to their visitors.

The People

History tells us that as early as Stone Age times a people called the Dakota, or Sioux (a shortened form of the name Nadouesioux, given by the early French fur traders) inhabited the valley. For centuries these people established a way of life as hunters and trappers as the area was abundant in wildlife. They were also successful fishermen as the lakes and the streams provided another plentiful source of food. And in the north country they harvested wild rice, which continues to be harvested today in many of the same regions.

History also tells of another people, the Ojibway (also known as the Chippewa). They were driven westward from their homelands around the St. Lawrence River valley by a more powerful and aggressive nation, the Iroquois. Because of the establishment of colonies in the northeast of the Americas by European traders and settlers, competition in that region resulted in Indian nations warring for territory. Thus, the Ojibway found themselves in the land of the Dakota. Having brought firearms and gunpowder with them, the Ojibway began to push the Dakota further and further from their original hunting and fishing grounds along the St. Croix. This eventually resulted in the Dakota nation leaving their ancestral homelands to follow the buffalo to the plains westward.

As the demand for land from the white man grew, the Ojibway disposed of their lands through treaty after treaty, signing away their children's inheritance. Presently, the Band of St. Croix Ojibway are located on reservations located near Danbury in northwestern Wisconsin and Mille Lacs in Minnesota.

The high demand for beaver pelts in France created a need for new trapping grounds as the eastern areas became scarce in this commodity. Thus, in 1679 Sieur du Luth and his party made an expedition to the northwest, as this territory was known then, and claimed this vast, unexplored region for his sovereign, King Louis XIV. Soon afterwards trappers, voyagers, and fur traders came, setting up fur trading posts along the Croix. Fur trading proved to be a highly lucrative industry and an important part of the history of the valley for more than a century. In the 1960s the Minnesota Historical Society reconstructed the Northwest Company Fur Post at its original site in Pine City, Minnesota. There you can see costumed guides reenacting scenes from the lives of the voyagers, trappers, and traders who once occupied this very space. A similar scene can be visited at Forts Folle Avoine, just four miles north of Webster, Wisconsin, on the Yellow River.

After the treaty of 1837 between the Ojibway and the existing federal government, this land was opened for settlement. Easterners came, attracted by the great stands of giant white pine. In fact, the lumber industry was largely developed by "New Englanders." The climate, soil, and opportunities here were very much like that of New England. Some of these early lumbermen became scions of vast lumber empires, establishing prosperous sawmills, and communities of charming rivertowns emerged. Many of the grand and historic homes of the valley were built by these same lumber barons. They were soon followed by farmers, central European and Scandinavian immigrants who heard of this richly fertile American valley available for homestead. They came by steamboat across the Great Lakes and up the rivers. Others travelled cross–country by prairie schooner.

The river transported logs and farm crops downriver to the growing towns of the Midwest. After the first decade of the twentieth century, all of the great white pine had been cut and the lumbermen looked to new regions farther west for their timber. There had been no replanting, no conservation measures to reestablish the pines, and so a vast wasteland of thousands of acres were left behind. The lumbermen are part of our past, but today many prosperous farmers remain in the valley, continuing to supply wheat, corn, dairy, and poultry products to the world.

Presently, the St. Croix Valley is an asset for its own sake, not because it provides any product for profit but because it enhances the richness of one's soul. Many find comfort and peace driving along a country road overlooking a bluff, finding a vista of the river that settles in your heart, one you can recall from time to time.

The Seasons

Some might be intimidated by our winters, but to those who respond to the white, glistening snow and clear, crisp chilled air, there is much offered in recreation in the valley. There are hundreds of miles of groomed cross–country ski and snowmobile trails in the state and county parks and in local orchards. One might even try ice fishing on the many frozen lakes. Although no claim to be any match for the Vail and Sun Valley enthusiasts, the valley does offer downhill skiing, especially fun for the novice.

Spring in the valley does not emerge all at once with a burst of color; it rather evolves. One looks for subtle hints: the return of nesting birds, longer and warmer days, the running of maple sap, the opening of the river, and the slow return of the grasses to their spring green color. Summer is a time of long, warm days and cooler nights—with a steady flow of visitors to the valley. Toward mid–September, as the leaves begin their transformation into a full array of autumnal beauty, the valley is at its peak of splendor. Throughout the seasons there are endless opportunities for recreation on the river, lakes, and streams of the valley, as well as in the rivertowns and nearby communities.

*Note — The following sources were used as a reference for this section:

Dunn, James Taylor, *The St. Croix Midwest Border River,* Minnesota Historical Society Press, 1979.

Washington County Historical Society, *Washington: A History of the Country,* The Croixside Press, Stillwater, Minnesota, 1977.

Left, 1884 Phipps Inn, Hudson, WI. (One of many historic homes).

Below, Hot Air Ballooning is a Valley favorite.

The Windmill Baldwin, WI.

Historical Outlines of Rivertowns and Beyond

AFTON
Situated between wooded river bluffs and the St. Croix River, the historic village of Afton was first settled by French families from the Red River valley in the north. These settlements were made at around 1837 near the mouth of Bolles Creek. Citizen Lemuel Bolles made a claim in 1843, and of historic importance built the state's first flour mill operated by water power. Around the same time two Yankee gentlemen, Joseph Haskell and J.S. Noris, also made claims and built their homes in the style of New England architecture. German immigrants settled in the 1860's and 70's, while the Swedish came later settling in the hills at around 1880. Today, Afton is a quiet residential community with a business district of quaint shops, restaurants and a wonderful marina.

Points of Interest—
Afton Historical Society – Located in the old village hall is a museum containing photos and artifacts of early life in the St. Croix Valley. Open Sundays, May-October 2:00-4:00 p.m.

Afton State Park - opportunities for hiking, cross country skiing, swimming, picnicking, and hike-in camping. For hours and fees call (612) 437-4359.

Carpenter St. Croix Valley Nature Center - Open daily to visitors 8:30 a.m. to 4:30 p.m. Public programs on weekends once a month. Miles of trails with beautiful views of the St. Croix. (612) 437-4359

BALDWIN
As early as 1850 Dutch farmers settled on the land which is now only a few miles from the present site of Baldwin. A gentleman by the name of Westendorp helped organize the settlement of which farming and milling were the primary occupations. At around 1870, former Vermont citizen, D.R. Bailey used his influence as a wealthy landowner, lawyer and community leader to convince David Baldwin, president of the West Wisconsin Railroad to locate the railroad directly through the Bailey farm. In turn, Bailey promised to donate twenty acres for the construction of a railroad depot and other maintenance buildings. Due to the railroad, Baldwin became a bustling hub of activity with such commodities as flour, butter and wooden shoes being shipped to the East and merchandise needed by the farmers and businesses came into the town by way of the railroad. During the early spring it's delightful to see the wonderful displays of tulip gardens put on by the area residents.

Points of Interest—
Windmill Park – A symbol of its Dutch heritage and of an authentic Dutch design is the windmill which sits as the centerpiece of Baldwin's Windmill Park. Three major festivals are centered at the park; "Taste for Tulips", "Let's Go

Dutch Days", and "The Festival of Lights". From Memorial Day to Labor Day a tourist information center operates seven days a week, 11 a.m.-5 p.m. in the windmill. (715) 684-3153.

HAMMOND
R. B. Hammond and other land speculators formed a company under the name of Mann, Hammond and Co. and bought up lands which had been set aside for schools and a university in St. Croix County. They encouraged people to settle and were successful in selling the lands, mostly used in farming. In 1856 the town of Hammond was established and named for R.B.Hammond. This farm community has maintained its tranquility over the past one hundred years.

HASTINGS
In 1819 a Lieutenant Oliver set up a cabin in what is present day Hastings and thereafter for many years the place was known as Oliver's Grove. The Dakota (Sioux) had always called it O-Wo-Bop-Te, meaning place where the turnip is. Then in 1853 a group of land speculators met to decide upon a new name for this rivertown. The names of three had been placed in a hat. Someone pulled the name 'Hastings' out of this hat and the rivertown officially began its life named for Minnesota's first Governor and one of the official founding fathers of Hastings, Henry Hastings Sibley. As a natural harbor site, Hastings sits on the banks of where the St. Croix and the Vermillion Rivers meet with the Mississippi Rivers. Thus, the town enjoyed being a distribution center for the logging, farming and steamboat industries. Many of Hastings' prosperous citizens of the late nineteenth century built splendid mansions and homes in the Gothic, Greek Revival, Italianate and Victorian styles of architecture. There are sixty-two properties in Hastings presently listed on the National Register of Historic Places. This rivertown, with recreational activities ranging from fishing to boating and swimming, is conveniently located just twenty miles east of St. Paul and is the gateway to the St. Croix Valley.

Points of Interest—
Spring Lake Park Reserve - Scenic picnic area equipped with tables, grills and drinking water. There are splendid hiking trails, and spectacular views along groomed ski trails for cross country skiers. In addition, unique to this park are the twenty two shooting stations comprising an archery trail of varying degrees of difficulty. (612) 437-6608

Walking Tour of Historic Hastings. Brochures for a self-guided tour of the historic district are available through the Hastings Chamber of Commerce and several of the merchants on Second Street. Included in the tour is the Hudson River Gothic style LeDuc-Simmons Mansion. The MN Historical Society is presently restoring the interior of the home which is a rare example of this style and detail. Plans are underway to open it to the public in the near future. Presently it can be viewed only from the outside. 1304 Vermillion St., Hastings. (612) 437-6775

HUDSON

Situated along the shores of the St. Croix River in Wisconsin, this historic river-town also found its past with many names - Willow River, Buena Vista and finally its present name Hudson. Named for the Hudson River as the area reminded one of its early founders, the city's first mayor, of his hometown river. Hudson developed rapidly as a lumber, railroad and steamboat center. Beautiful residences were constructed, particularly along Third Street, and remain relatively unchanged today giving us a glimpse into the past. Many of its past prominent citizens such as William Phipps, Hans J. Andersen, and William Penfield have made important and lasting contributions to society: Phipps Foundation and Center for the Arts; Andersen Window Manufacturing Corporation and Penfield's discoveries in neuroanatomy and function of the brain. As for recreational opportunities, Hudson's Willow River which empties into the St. Croix at Hudson has some of the state's best walleye and trout fishing.

Points of Interest—

The Historic Octagon House - built in 1855 for Judge John Shaw Moffat and his family, this house is a fine example of an eight-sided dwelling which was popularized in America during this period. This museum complex is maintained by the St. Croix County Historical Society and includes the home, gardens and carriage houses. The rooms are authentically furnished in period pieces and at Christmas time offers a grand display of traditional Victorian decoration. Listed on the National Register of Historic Places. Open May through October, Tuesday - Saturday 10 a.m. to noon, 2 p.m. to 4:30 p.m. Sundays 2 to 4:30 p.m. Christmas schedules are announced annually. 1004 Third St., Hudson, WI. (715) 386-2654.

Willow River State Park - Forests, lakes, waterfalls and panoramic river scenery are offered at this 2,800 acre park. Nature trails, campsites, lakes, boat launch, bath house, and beach in the summer months and cross country ski trails in the winter. (715) 386-5931.

Phipps Center for the Arts - Offers a year round season of theater, music and dance concerts as well as many special events. This $7 million complex houses a 231 seat proscenium theater and 125 seat black box theater. (715) 386-8409

PRESCOTT

Settled in 1840 Prescott is the oldest rivertown in Wisconsin. It is the place where the St. Croix River and the Mississippi River meet and the Wisconsin Great River Road begins. Indian agent Philander Prescott was sent to lay claim to this area in 1839. Because of its strategic location early speculators believed it was to become the greatest metropolis of the north; however, due to the greed of these early speculators in demanding large sums for land, St. Paul developed as the major city. In spite of this, Prescott did thrive as a community. Look for four historic murals in the downtown area that depict the past when logging and fur trapping were important industries for this town.

Points of Interest—
Kinnickinnic State Park. Fine Class A trout stream fishing, canoeing, swimming and overnight camping for boaters are available at this 1,067 acre park, most of which is only accessible to boaters from the backwaters of the St. Croix. (715) 425-1129

Prescott Beach - At the north end of the city on the St. Croix River there is a 400 foot stretch of beachfront with lifeguard on duty during authorized hours and offers swimmers such amenities such as toilet, bathhouse and drinking water.

Mercord Mill Park - At the confluence of the St. Croix and Mississippi. You can actually see the difference between the blue waters of the St. Croix and the brown waters of the Mississippi. A two acre park, with roofed picnic tables and grills offers scenic views. Amenities such as toilets and water are also available.

RIVER FALLS
Many New Englanders found similarity of place in this area as they noted the same pure waters filled with the same speckled trout, woodlands filled with the same sumac and elder. City founder Joel Foster settled here in 1848. A decade or so later River Falls was prospering in the flour milling industry. There were three flour mills and five grain elevators and a starch factory by the turn of the century. Remnants of the Prairie Mill can be seen today. As part of the Twin Cities Metro Area, River Falls has a present day population greater than 10,000 and is the site of the University of Wisconsin campus.

Points of Interest—
Walking Tour of Historic Downtown Area and Kinnickinnic River. Start at the Downtown City Park on this tour, which is primarily along the river and reveals its importance as the power for the milling industry. Obtain brochures from Main Street 2000 Project, Inc., 220 S. Main St., River Falls, WI 54022

A COUNTRY ROSE BED & BREAKFAST
Love of Roses Sets the Theme

Built in 1964 near Hastings, Minnesota, as an elegant family farmhouse for the Schneider family, this substantial home is situated on two hundred acres of the productive soil of the lower St. Croix Valley. Buster Schneider grows soybeans, wheat, and corn, while Helen, his interior designer wife, conducts the B & B, and tends the rose, perennial, and herb gardens.

As they found themselves with empty bedrooms after their children married and left home, the Schneiders, like so many of their counterparts, chose to do a B & B. Helen's theme of royalty and roses is illustrated in her use of names such as The King David Room, which is spacious, contains a king-sized bed, and has a private bath. Queen Jessica's Room likewise contains a queensize bed and has a private bathroom. Both guest rooms are splendidly decorated in soft, floral papers, and a mixture of country and antique furnishings. Fresh roses are placed in the rooms.

Helen takes pleasure in pampering her guests with complimentary baskets of cheese, snacks and fruit, and wine (or nonalcoholic beverage if you prefer). The country rose theme is carried through all phases of her service.

Breakfast is served in the sunroom and, weather permitting, Helen will set the table for breakfast in the gazebo.

You can enjoy a hearty breakfast of homemade goodies. Pecan-stuffed french toast is a specialty.

The Country Rose is at its best in June and the other summer months when Helen's rose gardens are in full bloom.

~~~~~~~~~~~~~~~~
THE FACTS
A COUNTRY ROSE BED AND BREAKFAST
13452 90th St., Hastings, MN 55033. (612) 436-2237.
Innkeepers: Buster and Helen Schneider. Established 1992. Open year round.
Rooms: 2 Baths: 2 pvt.
Cost: $85 double/weekends; $75 midweek. Cash/personal or traveler's checks.
Smoke free. AC. No children or pets.
Directions from Twin Cities: Take I-94 east to MN Hwy 95 south. In Afton, take County 21 south to 90th St. Right turn on 90th St. 2.5 miles to Country Rose.
~~~~~~

ROSEWOOD INN*
Enduring, Memorable and Romantic

In its pre-inn days, this stately natural brick Queen Anne mansion served as a residence to the Latto family of Hastings, Minnesota.

Bavarian immigrants, William and Marie made a great sum in rum bottling and later went into the banking business. The mansion was built in 1880. Much later the town used it as a hospital, sharing some of the history of its sister inn, Thorwood, also owned and operated by Pam and Dick Thorsen. At Rosewood they have created an ambience that invites romance. High ceilings, tall windows in grand bays, double parlors, one with a baby grand piano, one with a splendid fireplace, elegant furnishings, all elevate the quality of romance. Each of the eight guest suites are distinctive in decor, ranging from formal to exotic. What they share in common is that they are named for bodies of water near and about Hastings. Six of the suites have both fireplaces and double whirlpool tubs and this year Pam has added the Duxianna bed (A Swedish made bed of advanced technology) to the four top suites. A grand, gracefully curved, richly carpeted cherry and walnut staircase leads to the guest rooms. Each guest suite has a porcelain nameplate affixed to the door. Written on these nameplates are special messages of celebration, such as 'Happy Anniversary', etc.

If you are bent to the more formal you might prefer the St. Croix Suite. Originally the master's suite, the mahogany furnishings including a four poster bed and the lush green carpeting should be your style. This suite has both fireplace and whirlpool tub. My choice to fill most any romantic fantasy would be The Solarium. Described as 'sleeping in an outdoor paradise', you could be the god or goddess that occupies the room, which is filled with the splendor of vines and birds wistfully placed by tromp l'eoil art. To augment your paradise the fifteen foot high wall of glass allows optimum light to stream in. Of course this suite has both fireplace and double whirlpool tub. Moving to the exotic no one could forget Mississippi Under the Stars. Eight-hundred square feet under five skylights, fireplace, plantation teakwood double whirlpool tub, a delicately tiled shower-in-the-round, antique copper soaking tub, soft blues, burgundies and rich paisleys and exotic accessories create this splendid and luxurious suite. Inspired by the influence of Moorish designs in art and form that persisted in the late 1880's, the Thorsens took this theme all the way here.

Breakfast is served where you will; the formal dining room or your suite. Fresh fruit pastries, grapefruit flower, and generally the same menus are followed here as at Thorwood. The Thorsens also offer fixed price dining at the inn for guests only.

You can be sure all the luxury touches are here; scented soaps, plush towels, evening snacks and the Sunday morning paper to name some.

~~~~~~~~~~~~~~~~
THE FACTS
ROSEWOOD INN
620 Ramsey St., Hastings, Mn. 55033. 612-437-3297.

Innkeepers: Pam and Dick Thorsen. Established in 1989.
Rooms: 8 suites (6 with double whirlpool tubs and fireplaces. Baths: 8 pvt.
Cost: $75–$195/double. $15/add'l each person. MC/Visa/AE, money order
or personal check.
Smoke free. AC. No pets. Inquire about children.
Directions from Twin Cities: Take Hwy 61 south to Hastings. Turn left on 7th St.
and take to Ramsey. Rosewood is on the left.
*National Register of Historic Places.

~~~~~~

THORWOOD INN*
Respectable, Elegant and Romantic

Respectable, yes, because of the outstanding efforts of innkeepers and owners Pam and Dick Thorsen to reestablish this red brick French Second Empire home built in 1880 as an elegant mansion home. Their efforts included Dick's skill at recycling original materials from the home, replaning and reusing them in their restoration work. Originally constructed for prosperous lumber mill owners Sarah and William Thompson in historic Hastings, Minnesota, Thorwood proudly became one of Minnesota's first historic B & Bs in 1983. It has since established a standard for others to follow. Their philosophy was to create a place of solace from the 'warring battles of life'. Pam related that her best education comes from her guests and that they are responsive to guests' suggestions in continuing to create a place of comfort and solace.

Grand rooms with high bay windows, elaborate plaster ceiling moldings, and a classic marble fireplace in the main parlor characterize some of the fine features of this home.

All of the guest rooms are spacious, have queensize beds and private baths. The beds are covered with fine feathered comforters. Oversized, plush terry towels are used throughout. Some of the rooms have wood-burning fireplaces and Pearl whirlpool tubs. In all, there are seven guest rooms. Notable of these are Sara's Suite and The Steeple Room. Each of these suites have a distinct architectural feature. In Sara's Suite you encounter three levels of living space with the central focus an expansive high bay window. On the first level there is a cozy reading area with a daybed used for sitting. Level two contains the whirlpool tub and bathroom with a pedestal sink painted with violets. Above is the loft sleeping area, defined by a handsomely crafted wooden balcony in the gothic style. An iron and brass bed takes its place under the skylight. This is the suite most often selected by honeymooners, I am told. And so it is fitting that a German made antique musical wedding doll takes residence in this room. The distinction of the Steeple Room is just that - a steeple occupied by a whirlpool tub and fireplace which can be viewed from bedside or tubside. Buttons 'N Bows, on the first floor is handicap accessible through a ramp off the main porch.

Breakfast is served in the main dining room or in your room. Potato lover's omelette or Minnesota wild rice quiche might be your entrée. Fresh fruit might be topped with poppyseed lemon yoghurt and pastries are also served. Coffee or teas of your choice, of course.

Ask the Thorsens about their special Storybook dinners or popular hatbox suppers. They are happy to serve any need and accommodate business retreats, company parties and special occasions.

Guests are encouraged to explore some of the nearby parks for walking or hiking. Pam pointed out a collection of walking sticks in the entrance hallway that guests are invited to borrow for these sojourns.

~~~~~~~~~~~~~~~~

THE FACTS

THORWOOD INN

315 Pine St., Hastings, MN. 55033, 612-437-3297.

Innkeepers: Pam and Dick Thorsen. Established in 1983. Open year round.

Rooms: 7 (3 with fireplaces) Baths: 7 (4 with whirlpool tubs).

Cost: $75–$145/double. $15/add'l person. MC/Visa/AE, personal check or money order.

Smoking on outside porches only. AC. No pets. Inquire about children.

Directions from Twin Cities: Take Hwy 61 South to Hastings. Turn right onto Fourth St. Take to Pine. Thorwood is on the right.

* **National Register of Historic Places.**

~~~~~~

THE ARBOR ROOM
Private and Pampered Stay

This New England style home of the Arts and Crafts period circa 1905 was built by prominent banker Edward Longworth. The three lovely porches offer partial views of the St. Croix in Prescott, Wisconsin, just before its confluence with the Mississippi. River rocks from the St. Croix were used in the stone foundation. The ash woodwork and maple floors are complemented by the tasteful furnishings used throughout conveying an English cottage style.

Current owners Cyndi and Steve Schmitz were drawn back to the river after living in Florida for several years. An amiable couple who love people came naturally upon a decision to start a B & B. Hospitality comes easily to this pair, who pamper their guests with homemade chocolates, fresh flowers, down comforters and pillows, plush terry robes, and a choice of breakfast in bed, at the dining room table, or on the porch. Typically a breakfast might feature baked french toast, fruit-filled pastry, muffins, lean meat, and melon with sorbet to clean the palate.

Your stay at the Arbor Room begins with fruit juice and tasty treats reserved in a small refrigerator in the room. Impeccably appointed, this single guest room, with its private entrance off the arbor, communicates a sense of restful luxury. A bathroom attached assures privacy.

~~~~~~~~~~~~

THE FACTS

THE ARBOR ROOM

434 Court St. N., Prescott, WI 54021. (715) 262-4166.
Innkeepers: Cyndi and Steve Schmitz. Established 1990. Open year round.
Rooms: 1   Bath: 1 pvt.
Cost: $75/double. Midweek rates available. Cash/personal checks.
No smoking. AC. No children or pets.
Directions from the Twin Cities: Take Hwy 61 south to Hwy 10 east to downtown Prescott. On Cherry St. turn left to N. Court St.

~~~~~~

THE OAK STREET INN
One of the Oldest Homes in the Valley

Early settlers physician Orrin Maxson and postmaster William Copp had this Italianate style home built in Prescott, Wisconsin, in 1854. The home is not distinctly different from other Italianate style homes of the period except for its unique woodwork. Richly stained dog-eared shaped moldings are present on the windows and doorways of the main parlor. George Nichols, melodeon and pump organ manufacturer, lived here at one time, and the handsome pump organ that presently occupies the parlor was his creation. Serendipitously, inkeepers, Stan and Ann-Marie Johnson discovered it several years ago. Guests with musical abilities are encouraged to play.

It's plain to see this is a home by the carefully chosen family heirlooms and antiques used throughout the house. Young children live here, so there are no frills or extra flourishes. Homemade cookies often welcome guests. A walnut bannister leads to the second floor guest rooms, of which there are three. The original master bedroom, the Jenna Room, features a queensize bed, and a private bath with tub and shower. Another cozy little room adjoins containing a single bed for additional or separate sleeping quarters.

Avery is the name given to what the Johnsons call their "special occasion room." Handsomely decorated in shades of rose and deep blue with queensize bed, it has its own private bathroom with claw-foot tub and shower. A separate dining area allows for private breakfasts in your room. A gracefully decorated Elizabeth Room with a four-poster double bed and a separate area for dressing also has a private bathroom with tub and shower.

A full breakfast is served when guests gather between nine and ten in the morning; Ann-Marie sets the table with grandma's china. You sit down to a meal of pancakes and waffles with maple syrup, fresh fruit, juice, and coffee. Eggs, bacon, and sausage are sometimes served as a variation.

Common areas include a library and wicker-filled front porch. Ann-Marie is a past president of the Prescott Area Chamber of Commerce and has gathered lots of useful information, maps, and brochures for her guests to browse through or take as they require.

~~~~~~~~~~~~~~~~
THE FACTS
THE OAK STREET INN
506 Oak St., Prescott, WI 54021. (715) 262-4110.

Innkeepers: Ann-Marie and Stan Johnson. Established 1990. Open year round.

Rooms: 3   Baths: 3 pvt., with tub and shower

Cost: $75–$85 double, weekends. $50 double, weekdays with continental breakfast only. Discounts for multiple-night stays. MC/Visa/cash/personal checks.

Smoking in outside areas only. AC. Inquire about children. No pets.

Directions from Twin Cities: Take Hwy 61 south to Hastings, then Hwy 10 east to Prescott. Take Cherry St. to Court St., then left onto Court and right turn at Oak St. From WI: Take Hwy 35 to downtown Prescott and follow Cherry St., then proceed as above.

~~~~~~

INN ON THE HILL
Turret Room with Great Views of the River

Standing stately on a hill in Prescott, Minnesota, is this 1907 Queen Anne with northwestern facing turret. It was built by lumber baron George Hollister for his third wife Minnie Etta. Hollister so loved the Queen Anne elements that he incorporated them into this early twentieth-century home.

Proprietor Chris Samlaska had been a collector of antiques for years when he purchased this home with a view towards making it a bed and breakfast. Consequently, the Inn on the Hill saw its first guests in 1987. The home boasts of one of Pierce County's first homes with central vacuuming. Only one fireplace remains in the main parlor. Each room is graced by lovely stained glass windows. Of particular interest is the handmade "spider web" window in the guest room on the second floor.

The four guest rooms are creatively decorated, and each has a private bathroom. Some interesting features of the Spider's Web Room is the brass bed and full-size double shower. The Porcelain Room reminds you of Delft with its blue-and-white patterned paper and accessories throughout. In the Governor's Room you'll find a massive step-up four-poster oak bed, and the theme is carried to the whirlpool room with vanity table.

Guests are invited to the common area on the second floor called the Turret Room. Here a window seat in the round and splendid views of the river at sunset can hardly be matched.

A European style continental breakfast is served to guests as a basket of rolls, cheeses, salami, juice, fresh fruit cup, and coffee grace the table.

~~~~~~~~~~~~~~~~
THE FACTS
THE INN ON THE HILL

140 Locust St., Prescott, WI 54021. (715) 262-3986.

Proprietor: Chris Samlaska. Innkeeper: Jody Antoniou. Established 1987. Open year round.

Rooms: 4   Baths: 4 pvt., 1 with whirlpool.

Cost: $55–$85 double. Cash/personal checks.

Smoking restricted to designated areas. Inquire about children. No pets.

Directions from Twin Cities: Take Hwy 61 south to Hastings. Take Hwy 10 in Hastings east to downtown Prescott. Turn left on Cherry St. and right onto Locust.

~~~~~~
AFTON COUNTRY BED & BREAKFAST
Homey and Relaxing in the Country

After operating an executive maid service in the Twin Cities for thirteen years, Dee Cullen found another way she could be of service to working couples. She designed her present country home as a retreat to refresh body and soul. She and her husband are herb and organic gardeners and put great emphasis on healthful eating. They have provided a homey and relaxing place for their guests.

Take an herbal whirlpool bath in the Pink Room, which has a queen-size bed and large, comfortable sitting area by the fireplace. In the ivy-bordered Green Room, a country quilt covers the dark pine queensize bed.

You might want to try the tandem bike these hosts provide for their guests' pleasure. The country roads to town might be a merry journey.

Breakfast is served in the breakfast nook, which is surrounded by windows and hanging plants. A three-course breakfast is served here while you watch the birds busy at their feeders. All breads, waffles, muffins, and egg dishes are prepared from Dee's own recipes and organically grown ingredients. Fresh-squeezed orange juice is a nice surprise. If you prefer breakfast in your room, Dee will oblige with a continental style bounty.

Like a visit to Grandma's house, Dee wants to make this a positive experience for her guests. Since she loves to pamper them, one always leaves with a surprise memento. She recommends at least a two-day stay in the country. Her *bon mot*: "A day in the country is worth one month in the city."

~~~~~~~~~~~~~~~~

THE FACTS

AFTON COUNTRY BED AND BREAKFAST

Afton, MN 55001. (612) 436-6964.

Innkeeper: Dee Cullen. Established 1989. Open year round.

Rooms: 2   Baths: 2 pvt. (1 with whirlpool).

Cost: $60 & $90. Cash/personal or traveller's checks.

Smoke free. Barrier free. AC. Inquire about children. No pets. Call or write for directions.

~~~~~~

AFTON HOUSE INN*
History and Charm in Traditional Lodging

For more than a century, the Afton House Inn has provided traditional lodging and fine cuisine for the many visitors to the St. Croix Valley. Back in 1867 Charles C. Cushing built the inn as the second hotel in the town of Afton. A restaurant was added by "Mother Mary" Pennington when she took over in 1907. Her chicken dinners became famous in the valley, for she raised her own chickens out back and folks knew that meant fresh fixings. Several colorful owners followed, and then in the 1960's it ceased its function as an inn. Gordon Jarvis, who had a background in restaurant management, decided to purchase the Afton House. That was 1976. Together with his wife, Kathy, and mother, Betty, they pursued their dreams of reopening as an historic inn. Kathy persevered and obtained National Historic Register status for the original structure. They constructed an addition, and the total inn was reestablished in 1986.

There are fifteen guest rooms in the inn. Each is decorated with country wallpapers, and with original and reproduction antiques. All rooms have private baths. The deluxe rooms have whirlpool tubs and gas fireplaces. Room number thirty on the second floor contains a king-size brass bed and has a double whirlpool tub. A balcony overlooks the marina and St. Croix River. Room number forty-four on the first floor is a spacious room decorated with a cornflower blue country paper. It is furnished with a queensize white pine four-poster bed and two Queen Anne fireside chairs, and has a double whirlpool, gas fireplace, and private bathroom. Through a large patio door you have access to your private patio. Room number forty-six is handicap accessible and is a deluxe room also.

Breakfast is served continental style (juice, coffee, and rolls) daily to lodging guests. A full breakfast is available for an additional charge.

Three separately styled dining areas: The Wheel Room, features tableside cooking, The Pennington Room features a more private setting and the Catfish Saloon for a more casual fare; are open to guests and the public. Boaters are accommodated for an overnight dockage fee. Inquire about the many dining and pleasure cruise packages available at the Afton House.

~~~~~~~~~~~~~~~~~

THE FACTS

THE AFTON HOUSE INN
P.O. Box 326, Afton, MN 55001. (612) 436-8883.
Innkeepers: Gordon and Kathy Jarvis. Established l986. Open year round.
Rooms: 15, some with gas fireplace.
Baths: 15 pvt., some with whirlpools.
Cost: $60–$135. Cash/personal or traveler's checks. Credit card to hold reservation only.
Five no-smoking rooms. AC. Children welcome. No pets.
Directions from Twin Cities: Take I-94 east to MN Hwy 95 south to Afton. Continue to Afton House Inn, on the left in the heart of the town.
* **National Register of Historic Places.**

~~~~~~

RIVER ELMS CARRIAGE HOUSE
Private Retreat on the River

Driving through the white pillars posted on either side of the driveway of this private estate, you are impressed with the feeling of exclusivity. Kathy and Gordon Jarvis, owners of the Afton House Inn, are sharing this feeling with you as they have renovated the old, original cottage of this Lakeland, Minnesota, estate as a wonderful retreat, most exclusive and private. You enter your suite (the only guest room here) through an oak and beveled glass door; it is thickly carpeted. The many windows are covered with pleated shades that magically collapse into a delicate lacy covering.

The king-size brass bed is covered in an ecru, crocheted bedspread. The room is dominated by a six-foot round Jacuzzi with mirrored back splash. A gas fireplace is at the opposite end of the room, and in the corner is a cozy spot for dining for two.

Popcorn and nonalcoholic champagne awaits each guest, and continental breakfast fixings are left in the fridge for you to ready at your convenience. China, crystal and flatware are on the brass and wire rack and a fridge, microwave, coffee maker, and sink complete the conveniences of the kitchenette. There is a separate bathroom with shower.

Your hosts invite you to walk the grounds, and to use the beach and dockside. Other amenities include TV, VCR, movies, and clock radio.

~~~~~~~~~~~~~~~~~

THE FACTS

RIVER ELMS-CARRIAGE HOUSE
221 Lakeland Shores Rd., Lakeland, MN 55043. (612) 436-8883. Innkeepers: Gordon and Kathy Jarvis. Established 1993. Open year round.
Rooms: 1 suite   Bath: pvt. with Jacuzzi
Cost: $195 winter; $225 summer. Cash, personal check. Credit card to hold reservation only.
Smoking permitted. AC. No children. No pets.

Directions: Take MN Hwy 95 to Lakeland. When in Lakeland take N. 2nd St. east; it becomes Lakeland Shores Rd. Bear right and take a quick left onto driveway of River Elms.

~~~~~~

KNOLLWOOD HOUSE
The Good Life in the Country

Innkeeper Jim Tostrud grew up in this 1886 red brick farmhouse built by River Falls resident Sherlock Wales. Each of the bricks, I am told, came from the local brick factory that had operated in the mid-1800s. Jim pointed out some of the details of the home—the bird's-eye maple pocket doors, the trigger door mechanisms, and the cherry fireplace surround in the sitting room. His wife, Judy, an energetic woman, related that after touring England and staying at bed and breakfasts she decided to open one herself. In 1987 they started this enterprise and have been improving it ever since. Their philosophy is to offer the good life in the country while maintaining its charm.

And so they do. Apart from their four guest rooms, they offer a hot tub, sauna, swimming pool, mini-golf course (180 yards-par three), and hiking and cross-country ski trails. And if that's not enough there's more: an in-ground trampoline, lawn croquet, and badminton, to name a few.

Judy, an avid gardener for many years, has been successful at hydroponics and now has a perennial flower business. This is all evident as one enjoys the wonderful array of greenery in the solarium and lush flower gardens on the three-and-a-half acre lawn.

Recently the Tostrud's have remodeled their guest rooms to increase the pleasure of their guests. Christi-Ann's Room has a handsomely carved antique oak bed with matching dresser covered with an Amish quilt. Many family treasures enhance the room's charm. A private fifteen-by-twelve bath area separated by a screen is included in the room.

Across the way is the Sherlock Wales Room, which has a western theme. Jim, an avid fan of author Louis L'Amour and collector of Terry Redlin prints, chose this as a theme. An antique brass bed is offered for sleeping, and just below your window is a gently cascading miniature waterfall. This room may share a bath with the first floor guest rooms.

The third guest room on the second floor is the Country Rose. Here Judy decided to go for a more classic style with a four-poster queensize bed dressed in crisp white Battenberg lace. An antique oak armoire stands its ground against the forest green and mauve rose tones of the room. This room has a private bath with claw-foot tub and pedestal sink.

Downstairs the Garden Room offers a pair of Jenny Lind beds covered with Grandma's flower garden quilts. A half bath and private access to the plant-filled solarium, hot tub, sauna, and outdoor pool are conveniences. This is also available as a suite with the adjoining day room and front porch. Guests on the first floor can either use the shower on the sauna level or second floor bathroom. Thick cotton terry robes are supplied to guests for their comfort.

On the weekends, a full breakfast is served in the solarium among the greenery and will always include an egg dish, fresh fruit, homemade muffins and breads, juice, and coffee. On weekdays a European continental style breakfast is served. When in season, fresh strawberries and raspberries from the garden are added to delight you.

A sentimental favorite with the Tostruds is the buggy that Jim's mom rode to school as a child. Often guests take to sitting in it, and it makes for a great photo opportunity.

~~~~~~~~~~~~~~~~

THE FACTS

THE KNOLLWOOD HOUSE BED AND BREAKFAST
Route 1, Box 4, Knollwood Drive, River Falls, WI 54022.
(715) 425-1040 or (800) 435-0628.
Innkeepers: Jim and Judy Tostrud. Established in 1987. Open year round.
Rooms: 4 (1 can be a suite) Baths: 2 pvt., 1 shared. Extra shower.
Cost: $80–$95 double. $150 for suite—sleeps up to four. Cash/personal checks only.
Restricted smoking. AC. Children welcome. No pets.
Directions from Twin Cities: Take I-94 east to Hwy 35 south to River Falls.

~~~~~~

TRILLIUM WOODS BED & BREAKFAST
Country Home with a New England Quality

In May the surrounding woods of sugar maples, oak and ironwood are filled with trillium and other wild flowers. So Bobby and Milo Gray, your hosts, chose the name Trillium Woods for this contemporary Cape Cod home with a New England quality in River Falls, Wisconsin. Although both are midwesterners, the Grays have been long on admiration for New England. As an extension of their skills with people, and their love of decorating and cooking, they seem well suited to hosting a bed and breakfast. Bobby tells me that her philosophy is flexibility and being client focused.

The three guest rooms are contemporary country in design and each has a private bath. Bobby has used a variety of stencil designs throughout, which complement the artwork of such New England artists as Grandma Moses and Charles Wysocki displayed in each room. Queensize custom beds have been handcrafted by Amish artisans. There is a first-floor guest room for those with special physical needs.

Fresh brewed coffee and the morning paper greet you when you awaken. Guests are summoned to breakfast at nine a.m. and will enjoy a table filled with homemade *Aebleskiver* (Danish pancakes) accompanied with Trillium's own maple syrup, Danish fruit soup, coffee, teas, and juice. In fine weather dining might be on the prairie patterned deck overlooking the woods.

Great care has been taken here to create an environment that is pleasing, peaceful, and healthy. Walks on the fitness trails are encouraged for the spirit as well as the body.

~~~~~~~~~~~~~~~~

THE FACTS
TRILLIUM WOODS BED AND BREAKFAST

N7453 910th St., River Falls, WI 54022. (715) 425-2555.

Innkeepers: Bobby and Milo Gray. Established in 1993. Open year round.

Rooms: 3   Baths: 3 pvt..1 with whirlpool

Cost: $75–$95 double. $65–$75 double, midweek. MC/Visa/cash/personal checks.

Smoke free. AC. Inquire about children. No pets.

Directions: Take I-94 in WI to Hwy 35 south past downtown River Falls to 770th St. Then turn left, go to fork in road, and bear left to 910th St. Trillium Woods is on the right.

~~~~~~

THE BLUE BIRD COTTAGE BED & BREAKFAST AND RETREAT CENTER
Refreshment for the Body and Spirit

This contemporary home set in the rural district of Hudson, Wisconsin on a lovely wooded five acre site offers an opportunity for respite from the stresses of our modern lifestyles. Hosts, Laurie and John Flipse invite you to stroll their meadowland paths and leave your concerns behind you. Peer into the many nesting boxes which they have constructed and placed along the way, hoping that the resident birds have made use of them and you might find yourself "nose-to-beak with a baby bluebird, wren or swallow" as Laurie puts it.

You can stay in one of two rooms they have prepared for guests. The Crystal Room is radiant with early morning sunlight and contains a comfortable double bed for sleeping. The Violet Room decorated charmingly with these colors and so called, contains a queensize bed.

What's different about the Bluebird Cottage are definitely the hosts and what they offer as distinctly different for a B&B experience in this area. Both John and Laurie practice a lifestyle they call **The Art of Being**. They describe it "as a way to live joyfully in the presence of chaos and stress. It is a meditative art that uses classical music to assist in experiencing the True Inner Being of peace and love." While staying as a guest, you are invited to join with them twice daily in this art (between nine and ten in the a.m. and between ten and eleven in the p.m.).

Special dietary concerns are their concerns - no red meat is served. Careful planning and shopping at a nearby food cooperative brings many featured items such as; sugar free jams and jellies, sprouted wheat bread, muffins sweetened with maple syrup and barley malt sweetened chocolate chips. I sampled some of Laurie's cookies and they were delish.

Breakfast is served on the sun-filled screened porch or arrangements can be made to breakfast in your room. Entrées such as Tex-Mex omelettes, non-dairy soy-wheat crêpes and rye blend pancakes are successful with guests as are the turkey or chicken bacon and sausages. Fruits and beverages are served as well.

If you have always wanted to have your handwriting analyzed or an astrological chart this may be your opportunity. Laurie offers a free handwriting analysis (she studied an eighteen month course through the International Grapho-Analysis Society in Chicago, Illinois) or reading to her guests. There are many computerized astrological reports to choose from.

~~~~~~~~~~~~~~~~

THE FACTS

THE BLUEBIRD COTTAGE BED & BREAKFAST AND RETREAT CENTER
595 Boundary Rd., Hudson, WI. 54016. 715-749-4243.
Innkeepers: Laurie and John Flipse. Open year round. Established in 1993.
Rooms: 2   Baths: 1 full size - shared
Cost: $59–69 double - includes one free reading. Cash or personal checks.
Smoke free. No pets. Inquire about children.
Directions from Twin Cities: Take I-94 East to Wi. Exit at Hwy 12 and go south to County N, take a left turn on N and take to 90th St. Enter the first road on the left to the B&B.

~~~~~~

THE BOYDEN HOUSE
A Romantic Victorian Gothic

One is struck by the beauty of this Victorian Gothic home as it stands distinctive and yet harmonious to its surroundings on the corner of Third and Elm streets in Hudson, Wisconsin. Philo Q. Boyden, businessman, former mayor of Hudson, and author took particular interest in the construction of his home in 1879. It is no wonder, since the home when completed cost nearly $10,000, a considerable sum for that time. This two and a half story home continues to reflect quality as the magnificently carved black walnut staircase and other grand features of this home retain their integrity. Still standing in front of the house on Third Street is a good part of the original iron fence. There are oak and walnut inlaid floors. Between the parlors, there are high and wide arched doorways which had been featherpainted to mock burled walnut. A splendid marble mantled fireplace with a grand mirror hanging above is set off nicely with a graceful Victorian settee.

Your hosts, Julie Ayer and Carl Nashan, a cordial couple, are both violinists with the Minnesota Orchestra. Muffy, a very responsive pet dog, is their faithful companion. Julie often arranges Sunday soirées of chamber music and poetry followed by a reception. Carl creates extraordinarily beautiful stained-glass lamps which are seen throughout the home. My favorite is one which is set upon the dining room buffet.

Three welcoming rooms are offered for guests. The Boyden Suite, notable for its furnishings and size, contains a superb example of Renaissance Revival furniture in the antique walnut bed and dresser. A sitting room with accompanying daybed adjoins the bed chamber and a private bath with shower and pedestal sink also adjoin the room. There is excellent light in the Buena Vista room with its large bay window. Set in the bay is a crisp white wicker ensemble, decorated in blue and white as is the entire room. The brass and white iron bed fits well. Double and twin size antique walnut beds capture your eye in the Willow River Room. An oak rocker invites you to relax, perhaps daydream a bit. The bath chamber, a full size room containing a large clawfoot tub, old fashioned pull-chain toilet and antique dresser which serves as a washing basin, is shared by the Buena Vista and Willow River rooms.

Breakfast is served in the spacious dining room. Fresh raspberries, grown in their own yard, warm homemade breads and muffins, assorted fruits and a hot main course with choice of beverages is sure to satisfy. For their guest's convenience a refrigerator on the second floor is stocked with beverages.

This traditional bed and breakfast is decorated in authentic period antiques without having a museum quality. The emphasis is on comfort without stuffiness. Julie has accessorized with some of her favorite things which puts one at ease. Croquet and badminton can be played on the expansive lawn or you might be pleased by relaxing on the open front porch.

~~~~~~~~~~~~~~~

THE FACTS

THE BOYDEN HOUSE
727 Third St., Hudson, WI. 54016 (715) 386-7435.
Innkeepers: Julie Ayer and Carl Nashan. Established in 1990. Open: May thru Oct. (Thu.-Sun.)
Rooms: 3 Baths: 1 private and 1 shared
Cost: $75–$100 double. Cash, personal or traveler's checks
Smoke free. AC. Inquire about children
Directions from Twin Cities: I-94 to Exit 1 in WI. Take Hwy 35 N to downtown Hudson. Turn right on Vine and left on Third St. From northwestern or southwestern Wisconsin Take Hwy 35 to downtown Hudson.

~~~~~~

THE GRAPEVINE INN
Former Home of Andersen Corporation Founder

Coming to Hudson in 1896 after a series of unfortunate incidences, Danish immigrant Hans J. Andersen found work managing a lumber company, of which his father-in-law, Alexander McDonald, was president. Five years later he was doing well enough to build a ten-room home in the Arts and Crafts style on Vine Street in Hudson. This home's dining room was later to be the site of the founding of Andersen Corporation, largest window manufacturer in the world.

Avery and Barbara Dahl were thrilled when they had the opportunity to purchase and restore this comfortable home with its diamond-cut windows and tidy front porch. Barbara, an interior designer, decided on a "relaxed European country theme" for their bed and breakfast. She has been meticulously coordinating fabrics, designs, and furnishings for the rooms, which are named for French wine country regions.

The result is a delightful mix of very appealing and elegant rooms. The Champagne and Roses Room is decorated in navy, rose, and cream; it contains a gracefully carved antique walnut bed. Your bath in this comfortable room includes an antique soaking tub with shower enclosure, pedestal sink, and toilet.

French country is the theme for the room at the top of the stairs. Here, Barbara employed a special four-color paint technique and a stencil design to create the mood of country elegance. A queensize country French burled-walnut bed is dressed in a quilt of rich colored florals on a buttercream background. A private bathroom with shower and faux marble tiles accompanies this room. In process at the time of this printing is a Victorian country room that will include an antique, seven-foot-high back bed and matching dresser. The Dahls are planning to use rich jewel tones to create a mood of majesty. A private bathroom with whirlpool will accompany this room.

The Dahls offer guests tasty appetizers after check-in. Breakfast is served in the comfortable dining room. Enjoy their potatoe specialties at breakfast along with fruit topped with fresh cream.

A large, outdoor swimming pool is an added feature of this inn. And for your convenience, a full bathroom is located on the first floor for showering after a swim.

~~~~~~~~~~~~~~~~

THE FACTS

THE GRAPEVINE INN
702 Vine St., Hudson, WI 54016. (715) 386-1989.
Innkeepers: Barbara and Avery Dahl. Established 1993. Open year round.
Rooms: 3   Baths: 3 pvt.
Cost: $89–$119 weekends. Midweek rates $10 less per room. Cash/personal or traveler's checks.
Smoke free. Ceiling fans. Inquire about children.
Directions from Twin Cities: Take I-94 east to WI Exit 1,Hwy 35N. Take 35 N to downtown Hudson. Turn right onto Vine St. Take Vine to 7th St. From southwestern or northwestern Wisconsin: Take WI Hwy 35 to Hudson.

~~~~~~

THE JEFFERSON - DAY HOUSE
In The Heart Of Hudson

In the heart of Hudson, Wisconsin, there are two people responsible for bringing bed and breakfasts to that city; namely, Wally and Sharon Miller. Blend together this 1857 built Italianate home with its remarkable mid-nineteenth century features and the Miller's attention to detail and you have one very successful venture. Amos Jefferson one of the early dwellers of this home couldn't imagine it as it is today.

The Miller's have created four very private and individualized suites, and have taken their own experiences while staying in each room to provide their guests with the very best of conveniences. The tour begins as you ascend the gracefully carved walnut staircase to the second floor. Each suite has a double whirlpool and three have gas fireplaces. The St. Croix Suite, being the most deluxe has it all: sitting room, hanging chandelier over double whirlpool tub, gas fireplace, queensize polished brass and iron bed, large adjoining sunroom with dining area, and private bath and shower. Down the hall, the Harbor Suite decorated in soft primary colors of yellow, red and blue has a large double whirlpool tub facing the St. Croix River and offers the comfort of a queensize antique walnut bed. Enter the Captain's Suite and you notice a large portrait of an old sea-captain above the gas fireplace. The large antique brass bed and other furnishings of this room continue the nautical theme. A wonderful sun-filled room containing a double whirlpool tub awaits the guests of this suite. Private bath with double shower also available to this suite. To complete the tour of guest suites there is the Hudson Suite. A country theme dominates here, large oak bed with patchwork quilt and country memorabilia fill the room. Most unique is the loft bed over the whirlpool tub in the bath chamber.

Breakfast is served fireside in the dining room. Guests are privy to the next morning's menu so that they may have 'sweet dreams' of luscious fresh fruit, homemade muffins, ham, cheese or egg strudels, cherry cheesecakes or mocha tortoni. To further your delight, Wally, a choir director of thirty two years, sings a delightful song to finish the festa. Sharon would like you to inform her of your preferences or dietary restrictions. Full continental breakfast served on weekdays.

Your hosts also invite you to use their wonderful library which was added by the Day family, the second notable family to dwell in this house. Here you will find Wally's collection of Maxfield Parrish and Atwater Fox prints as well as his collection of Roseville pottery.

Wally and Sharon also offer the convenience of picking you up dockside at the Hudson marina should you arrive by boat.

~~~~~~~~~~~~~~~~

THE FACTS

THE JEFFERSON-DAY HOUSE
1109 Third Street, Hudson, WI. 54016 (715 386-7111).
Innkeepers: Wally and Sharon Miller. Established in 1986. Open year round.
Rooms: 4 (3 with gas fireplaces). Baths 4 with whirlpool tubs
Cost: $119–159 weekends. $89–119 weekdays. Cash or personal checks - No credit cards
Smoke Free, AC, Inquire about children.

Directions from Twin Cities: I-94 to Exit 1 to Hudson, WI. Take Hwy 35 north to downtown Hudson, take a right on Vine and left onto Third St. From northwestern or southwestern Wisconsin take Hwy 35 to downtown Hudson.

~~~~~~

THE 1884 PHIPPS INN*
Restored Elegance to this Graceful Queen Anne

In 1990 Hudson welcomed its third bed and breakfast, the historic Phipps Inn. This graceful and elegant mansion located on Third Street, one of Hudson's finest residential streets, was built in 1884 by Mr. William Henry Phipps, a prominent citizen in the development of this area. Mr. Phipps came to Hudson and prospered in many businesses, notably lumber, railways, and banking. He also served as mayor of Hudson. The Phipps family established a reputation for philanthropy, and the Phipps Center for the Arts stands as evidence of this today.

Cyndi and John Berglund carefully researched the concept of a bed and breakfast and worked through all the changes this lovely mansion underwent to provide its guests with the charm, restored elegance, and craftsmanship of the nineteenth century coupled with the luxury amenities of today. This is easily observed in the wonderfully refurbished seven original fireplaces with original Italian ceramic tiles and carefully carved mantles. The magnificent stained glass windows and graceful chandeliers provide sparkle against the richness of the parquet floors, oak wainscoting, and open stairway that leads to the guest rooms on the second and third floors.

Breakfast is served in the magnificent dining room on a banquet-size table set with fine china and crystal. On weekends breakfast is a full four-course event to include homemade pastries and other delectables. On weekdays guests enjoy a full continental breakfast.

The Bridal Suite delivers your dreams in the antique walnut half-tester bed, tile fireplace, and private double whirlpool bath. There are five other guest rooms to choose from, each with private bath. Four also have double whirlpools, and two have fireplaces.

On the main floor, you might choose to be entertained by the sounds of romantic or classical music as it is played on the converted 1920s Cable baby grand, which dominates the central parlor. A second parlor serves its guests as a game room, and yet a third more intimate parlor can be used for quieter moments. For the convenience of their guests, the hosts keep a fridge stocked with munchies and beverages on the second floor.

For those special occasions, Cyndi and John Berglund provide what is called the Retreat Picnic Basket. It includes two long-stem roses, a split of regular or nonalcoholic champagne, *assiette du fromage et fruit*, paté, a baguette, a decadent dessert, a box of gourmet chocolates, and a keepsake ornament. Cyndi and John are both enthusiastic and capable when it comes to recreating a sense of a genteel era past. They encourage you to enjoy their historic home.

~~~~~~~~~~~~~~~

THE FACTS

THE 1884 PHIPPS INN

1005 Third St., Hudson, WI 54016. (715) 386-0800.

Innkeepers: Cyndi and John Berglund. Established: 1990. Open year round.

Rooms: 6 (3 with fireplaces). Baths: 6 (all pvt.; 5 with double whirlpools).

Cost: $95–$159 weekends; $79–$119 weekdays.

MC/Visa/personal checks.

No Smoking. AC. Inquire about children. No pets.

Directions from Twin Cities: Take I-94 east to Exit 1 in Hudson. Proceed to downtown Hudson and turn right on Vine, then left on Third St. In northwestern or southwestern WI take WI Hwy 35 to downtown Hudson.

*National Register of Historic Places

~~~~~~

STAGELINE INN
Blend of Native American Heritage and Antiques

Located in Hudson, Wisconsin, on the old Stageline Road (the route travelled by stagecoaches from Hudson to Menominee, Wisconsin), this 1946 Cape Cod style home was built for a Mr. Robert Henderson who at that time was a vice president for the nationally known firm of Brown & Bigelow. A friend and frequent guest of the home had been American illustrator and artist Norman Rockwell, who was employed by Brown & Bigelow at the time as a calendar artist. The innkeepers have named a suite in his memory. This is a lovely four-acre site with a massive stone deck and barbecue area available for cookouts in summer-like weather.

Both guest suites are spacious, with private baths, and are decorated in the late Victorian style. Handsome beds are dressed in antique crocheted and embroidered linens, singular to this inn. Each suite has a private deck accented by a lovely garden space.

The overall style of the home is a very tasteful eclecticism. One of my favorite rooms is a small sitting area leading to the upstairs guest rooms. This area contains a collection of wonderful Indian blankets, paintings, Santa Clara and San Ildefonso pottery, and a magnificent example of the artistry of the Ojibway in a quilled-work cradleboard cover. Mission oak furnishings blend well.

In the wintertime, breakfast is served in a wonderfully large solarium adorned with the hosts' collection of Navajo rugs and other native American artifacts. A fine example of a Two Grey Hills rug can be seen here.

Your hosts Bruce and Bonnie Jones have thought of your comfort as they have prepared the guest rooms with all the amenities of home, including TV and radios. Bruce, a physics and chemistry teacher at a Minneapolis high school, together with his wife Bonnie, an artisan and antique dealer, enjoy preparing a full three-course breakfast that will include eggs Benedict or their special breakfast quiche, fresh fruits, muffins, and choice of beverages. They did mention that they would accommodate special dietary needs if requested.

~~~~~~~~~~~~~~~~~
THE FACTS
STAGELINE INN
451 Stageline Rd., Hudson, WI 54016. (715) 386-5203.
Innkeepers: Bruce and Bonnie Jones. Established in 1992. Open year round.
Rooms: 2   Baths: 2 pvt. Other amenities: Hot tub
Cost: $85 double. MC/Visa/cash/personal check.
Smoking in solarium only. AC rooms. Inquire about children.
Directions: Exit 2 on I-94 in WI. Go to traffic light and turn left onto Stageline Rd. Continue .25 mile to house.
~~~~~~

SUMMIT FARM BED & BREAKFAST
Simple Country Pleasures

This is a traditional farm home constructed in 1910 for the Hyde family, one of Hammond's earliest homesteaders. The Hyde's operated a 198-acre dairy farm. Until 1985 this home knew only one family; then Grant and Laura Fritsche tired of their urban lifestyle ensconced themselves in the country when they purchased six acres, a red barn, and the original farm home. Laura had grown up in Milwaukee, so she was a little hesitant about the isolation. Then she recalled her favorite stays at B & Bs and she thought, "Why not open our own B & B!" So after lovingly restoring this tidy home, they opened their B & B in 1992.

Guests are free to use the downstairs parlor, which is comfortable and remarkable for its honey oak trim, pocket doors, and window seat just below the oak stairway. The Hyde's are proud of the front porch, which seems just right for sipping iced herbal teas.

The two guest rooms on the second floor each have their own private bathroom. A double-sized antique maple bed and dresser with harp-shaped mirror occupy Mary's Room. The set is a family heirloom. Snugly fit into the room are a small table and chairs for enjoying a private breakfast. Across the hall is Jim's Room, which contains a high-back, white-painted iron bed; it is restfully decorated in soft blues. Both bathrooms have claw-foot tubs for lingering baths.

Breakfast is served in your room and sometimes, when there is a crowd, at the dining room table. Laura enjoys preparing what I called "Laura's egg roll-up" served with cream sauce on the side, a meat dish, breads, muffins, and coffee cakes. I had the opportunity to sample her tasty blueberry coffee cake with a wonderfully brewed cup of coffee when I visited.

Grant invites guests to roam about and enjoy the sheep, ducks, and pigs. Since he commutes some ninety miles to work daily, he finds this little hobby farm is just right for him.

~~~~~~~~~~~~~~~~
THE FACTS
SUMMIT FARM BED AND BREAKFAST

1622 110th Ave., Hammond, WI 54015. (715) 796-2617.

Innkeepers: Grant and Laura Fritsche. Established 1992. Open year round.

Rooms: 2   Baths: 2 pvt.

Cost: $45 single, $55 double. Cash/personal or traveler's checks.

Smoking in designated areas only. AC. Children welcome. Crib available. No pets.

Directions from Twin Cities: Take I-94 east to exit 65 in WI. Take Hwy 65 north 2 miles to Hwy 12. Turn right. Go 4 miles to 160th St. Turn left; go 2 miles. Turn right onto 110th Ave. Inn is on left .25 mile.

~~~~~~
THE KALEIDOSCOPE INN
Fascination with Kaleidoscopes and Antiques

Clint Andersen, owner of this classic revival vintage home in Baldwin, Wisconsin, wanted to bring his collection of fine antiques and kaleidoscopes to the enjoyment of many. In 1988 he purchased the home that was built in 1903 for Charles Settergren and family. Mr. Settergren, who also served as a realtor, was responsible for bringing many people to St. Croix County. Apparently the home remained in this family for nearly forty years.

Through his efforts, Mr. Andersen has restored the home to its former elegance. Apart from this fine example of turn-of-the-century architecture, a fine collection of period antiques is represented here with a splendid mingling of different styles such as rococco, Jacobean, classic Victorian, Empire, and oriental. Add to this a fascinating collection of more than seventy kaleidoscopes, and the environment is bewitching. From the moment you enter the reception area you may be entertained by the antique nickelodeon or a number of intriguing kaleidoscopes.

The diamond-shaped leaded glass windows, large oak pocket doors separating the front parlor and dining room, maple hardwood floors, open stairway leading to the second floor, and grand lighting fixtures are impressive. The feeling is carried to the guest rooms, of which there are four. Antique lighting fixtures, tall, ornately carved antique beds, an original Morris chair, and lace window coverings furnish these. Robes are provided for the three guest rooms, which share a large modern bathroom with tub and shower. The Blue Room has a pedestal sink for added convenience. A private three-quarter bathroom is part of the Rose Room.

Breakfast is served in the dining room; guests are summoned by the soft sounds of antique chimes. A full continental fare is presented with fresh fruit, cakes, breads, and a variety of muffins baked on the premises by hostess Cherie Jacobson.

Cherie tells me that the inn is exquisitely decorated during the Christmas season with antique ornaments and lighting. You leave the Kaleidoscope with a bit more knowledge than you had as you entered, as each guest is presented with his or her own kaleidoscope, printed with the history of this instrument.

~~~~~~~~~~~~~~~~

THE FACTS

KALEIDOSCOPE INN

800 11th Ave., Baldwin, WI 54002. (715) 684-4575.

Innkeeper: Cherie Jacobson. Established 1989. Open weekends October-May. Full weeks May-September

Rooms: 4   Baths: 1 pvt., 1 shared by 3 rooms

Cost: $55–$65. Visa/cash/personal or travelers checks

Smoke free. AC. Children welcome. No pets.

Directions: Take I-94 to Baldwin, WI, exit. Go north 1 mile to Curtis St. Make a left turn onto Curtis and take to 11th Ave. Located 35 miles east of St. Paul.

~~~~~~

Helen Schneider in her garden's gazebo at The Country Rose Bed and Breakfast in Hastings, MN.

The King David Room.

Rosewood Inn, Hastings. Queen Anne elegance.

Ball and Stick furniture make a lovely picture in the Music room alcove.

Pam Thorsen, innkeeper, carrying a hatbox supper to a guest.

Mississippi under the Stars Guest Suite.

*Thorwood Inn,
splendid
example of
French Second
Empire
architecture in
Hastings.*

*Right:
Pullman chairs,
the warm glow of
a fire in the main
parlor.*

*Left:
The multi-level,
Sarah's Suite.*

Guest keys.

The Arbor Room, a New England style Arts and Crafts period home in Prescott, WI.

Trillium Woods Bed and Breakfast, River Falls, WI.

Chas. Wysocki room of Trillium Woods.

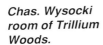

Left: The Oak
Street Inn,
Prescott.
Right:
The main parlor
note dog-eared
wood moldings.

The Inn on the Hill, Prescott, WI.

Spider's web
window of 2nd floor
guest room.

Massive oak four-poster bed in
Governor's Room.

Afton Country Bed & Breakfast. A comfortable spot on the front porch.

Breakfast in the country kitchen.

The Pink Room which has a whirlpool tub.

Kathy and Betty Jarvis, Innkeepers of the Afton House Inn.

Room No. 44 of the Afton House with its white pine four-poster bed.

River Elms Carriage House guest suite in Lakeland, MN.

The Knollwood House. An 1886 red-brick farmhouse in River Falls.

Christi Ann's room.

Solarium, where breakfast is served on the weekends.

Summit Farm
Bed & Breakfast,
Hammond.

Front porch.

Foyer and staircase.

The Bluebird Cottage Bed
& Breakfast, Hudson.

The Violet Guest Room.

Main parlor of the Boyden House in Hudson.

Boyden Suite.

Carl, Julie & Muffy on the front porch of the Boyden House.

One of Carl's beautiful stained glass lamps.

*Champagne & Roses Guest Suite of the Grapevine Inn,
Hudson, WI.*

The wicker filled front porch of the inn.

**"Former home of Hans J.
Andersen, founder of Andersen
Window Corporation."**

Morning beverages served to your room.

The Jefferson-Day House of Hudson. An 1857 Italianate home established as a Bed and Breakfast in 1986.

Whirlpool tub and fireplace in this romantic St. Croix Suite.

The Captain's Suite is dominated by an antique brass bed.

The music room
of the 1884
Phipps Inn
in Hudson.

Yards of lace on the
half-tester in the
Bridal Suite.

The magnificent dining room.

One of many stained
glass windows.

Stageline Inn, Hudson, WI - The Solarium.

The sitting room has a collection of Indian paintings and pottery.

The Norman Rockwell Room. Named for famed artist who at one time was a guest here.

The Kaleidoscope Inn - Baldwin. Named for the owner's extraordinary collection of kaleidoscopes.

The Rose Room.

The entry and stairway show off some of the antique lighting fixtures.

CENTRAL ST. CROIX VALLEY

The St. Croix as viewed from Pioneer Park, Stillwater.

Horse drawn sleigh rides just north of Marine.

Historical Outlines of Rivertowns and Beyond

HOULTON, WI

Located on the St. Croix River in St. Joseph Township of Wisconsin, this small community was previously known as St. Petersburg in the 1800's and is one of the oldest communities in the Valley. Mostly a farming community in the past; presently, because of its location on the river has been developing as a bedroom community for Twin Citians.

STILLWATER, MN

Located in the hub of the St. Croix Valley, Minnesota claim's the quaint rivertown of Stillwater as its birthplace. In the summer of 1848, the Minnesota Territorial Convention gathered here to inaugurate Minnesota as a separate territory. As the first official town site for the state, Stillwater broadcasts its other firsts as; the first county seat, builder of the first county courthouse, and home of the first territorial prison. Many of the St. Croix Valley lumber barons and highly prosperous entrepreneurs of the nineteenth century constructed their mansion homes in Stillwater. To name a few, John McKusick, Isaac Staples, George Atwood, William Sauntry, Jacob Bean, Samuel F. Hersey and Gordon Welshon. Fortunate for all, most of these mansion homes have endured and you will find a number of them among the list of Bed and Breakfasts of Stillwater. The town constructed a Grand Opera House in 1881 which hosted many of the best touring companies and exhibitions of the day. Destroyed by fire in 1902, what remains of the original structure is now occupied by Simonet Furniture Co., the country's oldest furniture store operated continuously by the same family. Stillwater continued to prosper in spite of the demise of the lumber industry in the valley. History reports this is largely due to the entrepreneurial nature of its citizens. Presently, Stillwater is headquarters to Cub Foods, Inc. one of the nations innovators in retail merchandising. Stillwater's Main Street is steeped in history with many of its original storefronts and warehouses still standing and now occupied by antique, specialty stores and fine restaurants.

Points of Interest—

Warden's House Museum - Built in 1853 as a home for the warden of Minnesota's first territorial prison, it served eleven wardens thereafter. The museum houses a large collection of pioneer artifacts, antique furnishings and is operated by the Washington County Historical Society which offers guided tours for a nominal fee. (handicapped accessible, first floor only). Open Tues., Thurs., Sat. and Sun. from 2:00-5:00 p.m., and by appointment. May 1 through Oct. 31. North Main St. (612) 439-5956.

Rivertown Restoration Inc. - It is a non-profit organization dedicated to preserving the historic resources of the St. Croix Valley. It sponsors a house tour each September and has published the Stillwater Walking Tour brochure. (612) 430-6233.

Washington County Historic Courthouse - Built in 1867 and used as a government center until 1975. Predominantly Italianate in architectural style, it is the oldest standing courthouse and jail in Minnesota. This National Register site offers a restored exterior and courtroom for viewing, rotating exhibits and rentals for meetings and receptions. Handicapped accessible. Tours by appointment, nominal fee. Open for browsing. Mon.-Fri., 9:00 to 4:00 p.m., 101 W. Pine St. (612) 430-6233.

Lowell Park - Established in the decade between 1910 and 1920, the park is located on the waterfront. Pavilion and picnic tables for your convenience.

MARINE ON THE CROIX, MN
Laid claim to by a group of twelve gentlemen, who had settled in Marine, Illinois, it was here the first timber was cut in the St. Croix Valley in 1838. These notable gentlemen Asa Parker, Orange Walker, Hiram Berkey, the three Judd brothers, Lewis, Albert and George, Dr. Green, Lucius Green, William Dibble, Joseph Cotrell, Samuel Berkleo, and Asa's brother James formed the Marine Lumber Co., which was to prosper for many years. A flour mill was established a little later by Dr. James R. Gaskill and the original name of Marine Mills was given to the town. From 1850 on, Scandinavian immigrants found their way to Marine and just a little north to the village of Scandia which was the first Scandinavian settlement in Minnesota. Evidence of these settlements still exist today in the museum at Gammelgarden. Toward the end of the century the lumber industry dwindled and with the popularity of excursion boats and the electric trolley, Twin Citians soon came to discover the beautiful St. Croix. American author, Sinclair Lewis wrote that "Marine is the most picturesque and beauteous spot along the St. Croix River." Folks began building summer homes and retreats in Marine. Much of the 'old town' remains as constructed over 150 years ago. The entire village of Marine is on the National Register of Historic Places.

Points of Interest—
Stone House Museum - Constructed in 1872 from local sandstone, the museum contains artifacts from early New England and Swedish settlers. Open Saturday and Sunday, from 2:00 to 5:00 p.m., July 4 through Labor Day or by appointment. Ann Ecklund, (612) 433-2061.

Gammelgarden - Located in Scandia, just a little north of Marine, this is the site of the first Swedish settlement in Minnesota. The eleven acre site houses six structures built between 1850-1880. The site is enclosed by Swedish log fencing. Celebrations include "Mid-summer" in June and "Lucia Fest" in December. Open May to October, Friday, Saturday and Sunday, noon - 4:00 p.m. or by appointment. (612) 433-5053 or (612) 433-3430.

Wm. O'Brien State Park - Camping and picnicking along the river, canoe rentals, boat launch, miles of hiking and cross-country ski trails, swimming, interpretive center, and nature programs. One of Minnesota's most popular state parks. Located just a little north of Marine on Hwy 95. (612) 433-2421.

OSCEOLA, WI

The name William Kent is known as the man who first laid claim to the Cascade Falls and surrounding area in 1844. Mr. Kent realized the potential use of the falls to power a sawmill. A small town grew out of this settlement and had several name changes until Osceola was finally chosen after the much admired Seminole Indian, Chief Osceola. As the lumber industry dwindled, farming became important to the economic base of the community. The power of the Falls was then used for milling grain. Milling continued on this site until 1919. During the 1860's German and Scandinavian immigrants came and established many farms. At one time Osceola had a steamboat manufacturing industry and a total of twelve steamboats were made here. The town depended upon steamboats coming up the Croix from St. Paul to bring needed supplies and export farm products. The railroad eventually made it to Osceola in 1887 creating a more dependable means for transporting goods and people up and down the river.

Points of Interest—

Cascade Falls - Located on the south end of Cascade St. you may experience the natural beauty of this impressive waterfall. Walk the foot-path that traces the old boardwalk to the falls.

Osceola & St. Croix Valley Railway - is a non-profit organization of the Minnesota Transportation Museum, the Osceola Historical Society and the communities of the St. Croix Valley to return passenger railroading to the St. Croix Valley. Board the train at Osceola Depot, just off Wisconsin State Hwy 35. Experience a twenty mile interstate round trip between Osceola and Marine on the Croix, MN. Weekends and Holidays-Memorial Day Weekend through Oct. 31. (612) 228-0263. Group or charter rates available (800) 643-7412.

COVER PARK MANOR - A BED & BREAKFAST
A Full Luxury B & B

It appears that when innkeepers are successful at what they do, they do it again—as is the case with Chuck and Judy Dougherty, owners and innkeepers of The Rivertown Inn in Stillwater. This time, a turn-of-the-century New England style cedar shake home with enclosed front porch and expansive grounds caught their eye. When this old Beach family residence (former landowners and blacksmiths) in Oak Park Heights, Minnesota, became available in early 1993, they saw an opportunity to bring yet another bed and breakfast to the St. Croix Valley. Thus, the story of Cover Park Manor begins.

The Doughertys create a wonderfully luxurious country inn with common areas richly decorated in period antiques. A country parlor invites you to congregate round the small parlor stove on chilly mornings. The first floor guest suite is constructed especially barrier free and offers the disabled easy access to bathroom facilities including whirlpool tub. A corner gas fireplace and double windows make this a more than sufficient room. Ascending the oak staircase to three guest suites, you find that all have private baths with double whirlpools and gas fireplaces. Paired windows, window walls, and skylights bring an abundance of light into the rooms, which are all richly decorated as a country manor might be. The family suite on the second floor opens to a spacious deck.

Refreshments and hors-d'oeuvres are provided to each suite in a hospitality bar.

Breakfast is served in the bright and crisp dining room and contains the same delights as the Rivertown Inn, as recipes are shared.

~~~~~~~~~~~~~~~~
THE FACTS
COVER PARK MANOR-A BED & BREAKFAST
15330 58th St., Oak Park Heights., MN 55082. (612) 430-2955 or (800) 562-3632.
Innkeeper: Chuck and Judy Dougherty. Established 1993. Open year round.
Rooms: 4 suites   Baths: All pvt. with double whirlpools
Cost: $129–$149 double. MC/Visa/Amex/cash/checks.
Smoke free. AC. Inquire about children. No pets. 1 guest suite barrier free.
Directions from Twin Cities: Take Hwy 36 east to exit for 95 south. Follow Beach St. to 58th St. and then turn right onto 58th St.
~~~~~~

THE ANN BEAN HOUSE
Landmark Home Warm and Friendly

This 1878 Queen Anne-Eastlake influenced home has always dominated the horizon of West Pine Street in Stillwater. It rises towards the sky, a majestic form with several towers seeming to almost pierce the clouds. Although massive on the outside, the carvings and details on the interior are graceful and refined. You enter through the etched glass foyer doors to a spacious reception area including a massive open staircase with intricate carvings. All of the oak woodwork in the form of trim, wainscotting, and mantels has aged to a mellow honey color. Extraordinary built-in leaded and beveled glass china cabinets are found in the formal dining room.

In its pre-inn days, this mansion home served as residence of lumber baron Jacob Bean and his wife Cynthia; they purchased it in 1880. It remained a family home for many decades, passed down to daughter Ann and her husband Albert J. Lehmicke, a prominent Stillwater banker. In the 1950s, Ann's oldest son Eugene converted it into eight apartments, while carefully preserving the details of the home.

Bruce and Victoria Brillhart purchased the home in 1990 and undertook the mammoth task of restoring this mansion to its former splendor. After a year of laborious restoration, including the removal of many layers of wallpaper and paint, The Ann Bean House opened to its first guests in 1991.

Upon checking in, you are greeted by Bruce and Vicki, who are friendly and attentive as they preside over the hospitality hour when treats and wine are served. Vicki instantly makes you feel comfortable and welcome even though some of us may have never dreamed of stepping into a home such as this.

All five of the guest rooms are beautifully decorated and have private baths. You might have selected one of the two tower rooms, each being distinctly different in mood. If you did, you would find the Tower Room on the third floor with its delicate pink lacy wreath paper and intricately curved antique white iron bed. A breakfast nook is tucked in the tower. Stairs leading up to the very pinnacle of the house end with fantastic views of Stillwater and the river. A fantasy fulfilled!

Across the way is the east tower room, Cynthia's Room being the formal name. Here you are reminded of a refined elegance with a lush mauve carpet underfoot acting as a stage for the brass and iron bed, exquisite wallpaper, and gracefully curved Victorian settee upholstered in a velvet celadon. A charming table with balloon-back chairs sits under the north facing tower window with its partial view of the river. A richly stained reproduction mantel surrounds a woodburning fireplace, and a bathroom containing a whirlpool in the round are wonderful.

The second floor guest rooms are spacious and wallpapered in document papers. Fine antiques and high windows allowing soft light to come into the rooms add to their charm.

A three-course breakfast is served in the dining room, which has a wonderfully carved oak mantel and sparkling oak floors. You might have breakfast in bed with fresh pastries, bread, homemade jellies, and coffee.

At the writing of this book the formal parlor was in the process of restoration. But from what I've seen it promises to be grand.

~~~~~~~~~~~~~~~~

THE FACTS

THE ANN BEAN HOUSE
319 W. Pine St., Stillwater, MN 50082. (612) 430-0355.
Innkeepers: Bruce and Victoria Brillhart. Established 1991. Open year round.
Rooms: 5, 2 with fireplaces. Baths: 5 pvt., 2 with whirlpools.
Cost: $95–$130 dbl, weekends. $75–$110 dbl, midweek. MC/Visa/cash/personal checks.
No smoking except on porch. AC. No children or pets.
Directions from Twin Cities: Take Hwy 36 east to Greeley St. in Stillwater. Go north on Greeley to Pine. Turn right on Pine.

~~~~~~

BATTLE HOLLOW BED & BREAKFAST
Simple Grace and Elegance Fitting a Queen Anne

The grace and elegance of this late Queen Anne-Craftsman home built in 1890 by Mr. John McKusick, first mayor of Stillwater, is evident both inside and outside. With its large open porches, lovely gardens, fine antiques, rich oak floors and woodwork, and open floor plan, this home is most gracious.

Innkeepers Beth and Jeff Griffith have looked after every detail of this wonderful restoration and performed most of the labor themselves. The soft, pale yellow color accented with green they have chosen for the exterior of the house lends to its grace. Battle Hollow takes its name from a well-known Indian battle fought in 1839 between the Ojibway and Dakota that took place in the ravine just below the house.

Both guest rooms have a lovely view of the river in the late fall and winter. Ella's room bears its name for John McKusick's daughter, Ella McKusick Merry, for whom the house was built as a wedding present. Its high window bay, large Victorian mirrored walnut armoire, and iron and brass bed make this a winsome room. The room has its own private bath and a gas fireplace as additional features.

Beth, although busy as a full-time nurse at a nearby technical school, has found the time to make the wonderful draperies, other window treatments, and duvet covers for the down comforters. In the summertime when Beth is not working at her full-time job, she enjoys innkeeping and provides great service to her guests, as is evidenced in the extra-thick plush towels, fresh cut flowers in all the rooms, and soaps from the Provencé in France.

Breakfast is served at your convenience in the lovely dining room. It usually consists of fresh fruits, berries, home-baked muffins, a hot entrée such as potato egg souffle, and your choice of beverages. And to keep you up-to-date, there's a complimentary morning paper.

Guests are invited to enjoy the impeccably decorated first floor with its main parlor and fireplace, library for relaxing with your favorite book, or music room if you are inclined to play the baby grand. The lovely two-acre site is a welcoming place for walks or sitting out back. One can walk easily to downtown Stillwater.

~~~~~~~~~~~~~~~~~~

THE FACTS

BATTLE HOLLOW BED & BREAKFAST

903 N. Fourth St., Stillwater, MN 55082. (612) 430-8001.

Innkeepers: Beth and Jeff Griffith. Established: 1991. Open all week June-August; weekends only September-May.

Rooms: 2 (1 with fireplace). Baths: 2 pvt.

A third room is planned for winter '93.

Cost: $95–$105. Reduced midweek rates. Cash/personal check only.

Smoke free. AC rooms. Inquire about children.

Directions from Twin Cities: Hwy 36 east to downtown Stillwater, left onto Myrtle St., then right on N. Fourth. From I-94: Take MN Hwy 95 north 10 miles to downtown Stillwater.

~~~~~~

THE BRUNSWICK INN
Gourmet's Delight in Town's Oldest Structure

Don't be surprised if there is a tilt to the floors here and there in this surviving old frame structure. Dating back to 1848 (the same year the village of Stillwater was surveyed and platted), the Brunswick Inn, as it is known today, was built by Julius Brunswick. He operated a mercantile establishment from the first floor while he and his family lived upstairs. The Greek Revival structure withstood the infamous mudslide of 1852 and has been restored to the mid-Victorian era in character and decor by Duane and Martha Hubbs, who are the same husband and wife team that have gloriously restored the William Sauntry Mansion on North Fourth Street in Stillwater.

The three guest rooms on the second floor are named for three of the Brunswick sisters. Each room is carpeted and has a woodburning fireplace and double whirlpool with private bath. Miss Anna's Room, papered in a cinnamon-pumpkin swirl and paisley design, offers an antique high-back oak double bed; it is dressed in a richly colored quilt. The rooms named for Emma and Amelia, the more soft-spoken and feminine sisters, reflect that nature. An unusual, mirrored-back mahogany headboard with applied carving is remarkable in Miss Amelia's Room. Breakfast is served in the rooms as the guests seem to prefer privacy here. A full three-course breakfast with fruits and breads and beverages is brought in a basket to your room.

This wonderfully restored inn has an elegant dining room devoted to Victorian traditions. The three separate chambers speak of a refined decor and intimate mood. Dinner is served twice weekly, on Friday and Saturday night. Just one seating nightly is available, so reservations are absolutely necessary. This is a five-course dining experience with fixed menu and fixed price of $29.50 per person. The menu, which changes monthly, might feature such dishes as crab strudel, herbed vegetable crépes, house salad, stuffed chicken breast, and chocolate marquise. All of this is served on fine imported china and damask table linens by the soft glow of candlelight.

~~~~~~~~~~~~~~~~~~

THE FACTS

THE BRUNSWICK INN

114 E. Chestnut St., Stillwater, MN 55082. (612) 430-2653.

Innkeepers: Duane and Martha Hubbs. Established 1992. Open year round.

Rooms: 3 with fireplaces. Baths: 3 pvt. with whirlpools.

Cost: $129–$139. MC/Visa/Amex/cash/personal or traveler's checks

Smoke free. AC. No children or pets.

Directions from Twin Cities: Take Hwy 36 east to downtown Stillwater, where it becomes Main St. Take a left onto Chestnut. Parking is provided adjacent to the inn.

~~~~~~

THE ELEPHANT WALK - A BED & BREAKFAST
A Blend of Three Cultures in a Vintage Victorian

Announce your arrival at the Elephant Walk with the sound of a Burmese temple gong, which is attached outside near the front door of this bed and breakfast. Jon and Rita Graybill, who have spent more than twenty years in the diplomatic service, decided upon this stick style vintage 1883 Victorian in Stillwater for their home and realized a dream when they completed its restoration and then transformed it into a bed and breakfast.

This lovely home was constructed for John Cesar, known to be Stillwater's first jeweler. The screened wraparound porch and scale of rooms compliment a most distinctive blend of artifacts of different cultures, namely Far Eastern, Spanish, and American. Rita has an unimpeachable sense of decorating style and manages to intrigue, entertain, and charm with her layers of object d'art.

An original bamboo four-poster queensize bed was designed and constructed by Rita for the Raffles Room. She hand tied the bamboo posts together with raffia cord and decorated the canopy with netting. Those of you who are mystery fans might remember the amateur cracksman A. J. Raffles from the E. W. Hornung stories. But Jon tells us that the room takes its name from the Raffles Hotel in Singapore. A gas fireplace adds warmth and a private bath with antique claw-foot tub and shower to increase your pleasure.

Handsomely decorated, the Rangoon Room is on the main floor. There is a remarkable nineteenth-century handcarved teak four-poster bed with brass accents that has been brought from Burma and now offers the opportunity for one to sleep upon it in Stillwater. To accompany this wonderful bed are an antique Spanish writing desk and armoire. The private bathroom with shower is decorated whimsically in costumes and masks from Bali.

Last in this tour of guest rooms is the large Cadiz Suite on the second floor. Cadiz, Spain, is the port from which Christopher Columbus set sail on his discovery tour. Here you will discover ancient hand-carved cathedral doors from that city, a large Spanish armoire, and a Persian carpet. The adjoining sunroom, with its flower-filled paper and bountiful hanging plants, feels like a garden. The feeling of eternal summer is created as sunlight forever streams in through the windows. A private toilet and shower are also in the suite.

Planned for the fall of 1993 is the Chaing Mai Room. This room will have a fireplace and private bathroom. The theme is set to celebrate the textiles and baskets made by the Thai hill tribe known as Chaing Mai.

Breakfast is served when Rita sounds the gong, a surprisingly gentle sound from the antique Burmese dragon standing in front of the dining room windows. Your breakfast might be a puffed omelette served with vegetables, fresh fruit cup, herbed popovers, heart-shaped scones, and choice of beverages.

Weather permitting, enjoy the flower gardens or make yourself comfortable in the main sitting area among fascinating objects that all seem to have a story. Your hosts Jon or Rita would be delighted to tell you and add a memory or two from your stay at the Elephant Walk.

~~~~~~~~~~~~~~~~~
THE FACTS

THE ELEPHANT WALK

801 W. Pine St., Stillwater, MN 55082. (612) 430-0359. Established 1992. Open year round.

Rooms: 4 (1 on first floor). Baths: 4 pvt. Cost: $99–$115 dbl.

Reduced midweek rates & business rates. MC/Visa/personal check.

Smoke free. AC rooms. No children or pets.

Directions from Twin Cities: Hwy 36 east to Greeley St. North on Greeley to Pine. Make a right turn. From I-94: Go 10 miles north of MN Hwy 95 to 36, then west to Greeley.

~~~~~~

THE HEIRLOOM INN
A Quiet Romantic Inn

Built in the late 1860s in Stillwater by Swedish craftsmen, this lovely Italianate style Victorian home was first occupied by Mr. William Bell. At the time it boasted a "state-of-the-art" coal-burning furnace using the principle of "gravity heating." The Bell family lived here for several years, and the home was then sold to Stephen Clewell. Thereafter not much is known about past ownerships.

The house has survived unmuddled. The interior is relatively original in scale and features. There are wonderful, large arched pocket doors between the front parlor and the sitting room. Masterful feather painting has been employed to fool the eye into believing that burled walnut has been used throughout as woodwork instead of white pine, which was so plentiful at that time. Just off the dining room is a large screened porch just right for quiet moments and contemplation. The upstairs has three guest rooms furnished with large, comfortable antique beds. The largest suite has a sitting room and spacious bath with a lovely old soaking tub with old brass fixtures and a hand-held telephone shower.

The entire home is furnished with appointments of the period, many of which are family heirlooms. The owners have accomplished setting a quiet, romantic mood of a century past.

Mark and Sandie Brown, your hosts and innkeepers, have been bed-and-breakfast adventurers for many years. Whenever they have travelled across the country, they have sought out accommodations in bed and breakfasts as their preference. So in 1988, when they had the opportunity to purchase the residence at 1103 South Third Street, it followed what they should do with this impressive residence. After careful planning, restoration of the original scale of rooms, and decorations, they opened their home as a guest house. Today, it is the second oldest bed and breakfast in continuous operation in Stillwater. Mark and Sandie consider themselves the concierge. They have learned from their experiences what guests expect and enjoy. They do their utmost in permitting guests to be as creative as they want to be in using their home for special purposes. An example of this is setting up their parlor for a proposal of marriage in front of the warmth of a fire and candlelit room.

Candlelit breakfasts in the dining room, with Mark playing classical music on their baby grand, is a bonus you will enjoy at this restful and gracious home. Some of the food offerings, all prepared on site, are hot, individual quiches, fruit of the season, muffins, rolls, and choice of beverage.

Sandie, a soft-spoken woman, is enamored with making bibelots from her collection of many small, interesting bottles. I'm left with the impression that you might be the recipient of some special treat after leaving here as a guest.

~~~~~~~~~~~~~~~~

THE FACTS

THE HEIRLOOM INN

1103 S. Third St., Stillwater, MN 55082. (612) 430-2289.

Innkeepers: Mark and Sandie Brown. Established: 1989. Open year round (except Christmas eve and day).

Rooms: 3   Baths: 3 pvt.

Cost: $85 double. Midweek discounts. Cash or personal checks only.

Smoke free. AC. Inquire about children.

Directions from Twin Cities: Take Hwy 36 east to Osgood, then go north to Burlington St. Take a right turn to Third St. From I-94: Take MN Hwy 95 north 10 miles to 36, and then take 36 west to Osgood.

~~~~~~

JAMES A. MULVEY RESIDENCE INN
Remarkable Examples of Craftsmanship

Shortly after the Civil War, a young man returned to his hometown carrying with him a handful of black walnuts. He married, made his fortune in lumber, and built his family a grand home in the Italianate style. On the grounds he planted his walnuts, and from them grew black walnut trees that are mature and flourishing today. That man was James A. Mulvey, for whom this residence is named.

Your innkeepers, Truett and Jill Lawson moved to Stillwater in 1990 and found this wonderful home in less than reverent condition. However, they did come upon an uncommonly important and wonderful fireplace created by the Grueby Tile Co. of Boston. The creation dominates the double parlor and is the work of architect A. B. LeBontellier. There is a frieze of landscape tiles at the top called "The Pines," most likely painted in this fashion to reflect the prosperous white pine industry of the valley. How fitting for the Lawsons, eminent collectors of nineteenth-century Rookwood pottery and other ceramics, to have this home.

The romantic Grueby Room is on the main floor and contains a lovely queensize polished brass bed and soaking tub. A private toilet and sink are part of this suite. On the second floor you'll find the Moorcroft Room with its delicately stencilled garlands and antique mahogany four-poster canopied bed. A lovely tiled bathroom and shower accompany this room. The innkeepers are proud of their sunfilled Rookwood Room, which overlooks the side yard; it is furnished with massive walnut Renaissance Revival bed and matching chest and dresser. Private tiled bathroom with shower in this suite.

Breakfast is served in the Arts and Crafts dining room, and Jill and Truett enjoy preparing a four-course eventful repast of Swedish pancakes with fresh orange glaze and raspberry streusel muffins; they always finish with chocolate-covered strawberries.

The Lawsons have created a most comfortable bed and breakfast with many amenities, including a turndown service and mountain bikes to be used for your pleasure.

~~~~~~~~~~~~~~~~

THE FACTS

THE JAMES A. MULVEY RESIDENCE INN

622 W. Churchill St., Stillwater, MN, 50082. (612) 430-8008.

Innkeepers: Truett and Jill Lawson. Established: 1992. Open year round.

Rooms: 5 (1 on first floor). Baths: 5 pvt.

Cost: $89–99 double. Midweek rates available. MC/Visa/personal check.

Smoke free. All AC. Inquire about children.

Directions from Twin Cities: Hwy 36 east to Greeley St. in Stillwater; take it north to Churchill where you make a right turn. From I-94: Take Hwy 95 to junction of Hwy 36; go west to Greeley Street.

~~~~~~

THE LAUREL STREET INN
Restored, Romantic River Inn on the Bluff

Eminently positioned on one of the high bluffs overlooking Stillwater and the St. Croix, this elegantly restored 1857 residence creates a beautiful picture for all who chance by. For three years Clyde and Mary Jorgenson have been putting all their resources into this historic site. Originally built for Judge Hollis Murdock and family, most likely as a farm residence, the Jorgensons purchased it in 1990. Clyde's expertise in the construction industry led him to undertake the project.

An old neglected barn that formerly stood on the property was torn down and made space for a large, well-planned addition, which carefully matches the character of the original structure. The limestone foundation blocks were reused in the retaining walls in the garden areas.

At the main house, well-crafted beechwood bookcases and mantels, stairways, windows, hardware, and doors from the earlier home were fit back in to retain some of the integrity of that first house. The results are splendid, as they have taken this nineteenth-century home well into the twentieth century. As further evidence of this, Clyde's company, inventors of In-Floor heating systems, has had this system installed in all walkways and driveways, and as the main heating system of the entire home.

The tiered gardens are fine for walking and enjoying the outstanding vistas of the river and of Stillwater. The gardens receive special attention from both Clyde and Mary. They decided to share their special home with guests after having had many positive and fond memories from their bed and breakfast experiences. Clyde particularly "fell in love" with Stillwater, which he says is "a wonderful retreat from the cities". The Jorgensons plan to provide a tandem bike for their guests.

Mary especially enjoyed furnishing and decorating the three guest suites. On the first floor, you enter the Murdock Suite, crisply decorated in verdant greens and white. After cleaning the slate that surrounds the hearth of the corner fireplace, they found it had a greenish cast, which set the tone for this room. A finely fabricated queensize, wrought iron bed occupies the main wall. It is canopied, and dressed with a handmade quilt, lace, and ivy. A wicker table and chairs sit in the bay. Through lace-curtained French doors you enter the bath chamber, which contains whirlpool, vanity, and toilet. Floral-patterned, cornflower blue plush carpeting leads up the stairway to the second floor rooms.

At one time, children's book author Mildred Comfort lived in this house (1914-1920). The name of one of the upstairs suites, Millie's Room, marks that heritage. The colors of lilacs and tea roses, found in the English art nouveau tiles surrounding the hearth of the newly installed white-mantled gas fireplace, set the theme of the room. White wicker accents and painted white window frames and moldings keep the room restful.

Across the hall is the St. Croix Room. Here English tiles depicting birds of the marsh surround the hearth of the gas fireplace. The soft, rich tones of the tiles are echoed in the room, creating a placid quality reminiscent of the river St. Croix, which you can watch from this room. Both second floor rooms have queensize beds with pillow top New Zealand wool mattresses. Each room has a private bathroom with whirlpool.

Along the walls of the hallways and stairway are Mary's collection of framed period wedding photos, hopefully inspiring to visitors of the inn.

Breakfast is served in your room, at your convenience, and will include fresh baked goods, fresh fruit, and choice of beverages.

Following the arches of the front doors, the Jorgensons have added a double arch leading to the parlor, which retains the judge's original library bookcases and is richly furnished with comfortable sofa and chairs. Here guests can come together to enjoy fruit and cheese plates and Mary's mandarin orange cake bars while they feel the warmth of a fire or gaze over the river and its activity. The doorway off the parlor opens onto the veranda facing the riverside.

AM-FM radio cassette players, fresh flowers, and a Bunny-by-the-Bay creation are present in each room. Guests can meander down just 101 steps to the Warden's House Museum in downtown Stillwater or take the tandem bicycle for an adventure in town.

~~~~~~~~~~~~~~~~
THE FACTS

THE LAUREL STREET INN
210 East Laurel St., Stillwater, MN 55082. (612) 351-0031.
Innkeepers: Clyde and Mary Jorgenson. Established 1993. Open year round except for the Christmas season.
Rooms: 3 with gas fireplaces. Baths: 3, all with whirlpools
Cost: $100–$140 double. MC/Visa/cash/personal or traveler's checks.
Smoke free. AC. No children or pets. Note: 1st floor is accessible through the rear for those who can't walk the front steps.
Directions From Twin Cities: Take Hwy 36 east to Stillwater. Take Second St. north to Laurel. Inn is next to Pioneer Park.

~~~~~~

LOWELL INN
Ornament to the City of Stillwater

The sixty-four-year-old Lowell Inn, a three-story red brick Colonial style hotel, with twenty-one guest rooms and three dining rooms, sits on the hillside in the heart of the City of Stillwater as a proud ornament of its past and present day's allure. It was only fitting that this structure was made to be reminiscent of the early history of America. The settling of this area has been rooted in the eastern states, and the thirteen stately white pillars fronting this edifice proudly declare the memory of the thirteen original colonies. The Lowell Inn has been named for former hoteliers, the Lowells, whose son Elmore donated the land for development of a new hotel on the site of the old Sawyer House. Since 1929 when Nelle and Art Palmer, Sr., took possession of the Lowell Inn, it has maintained its renowned reputation for quality, service, and tradition. Art Jr., as he is affectionately known, present-day owner and innkeeper, proudly tells the story of his mother Nelle's eccentricities and how her style of dress and manner attracted dining guests to the inn. Her elegant portrait hangs in the Georgian style lobby, and it is clear what a fine figure of a woman she was.

As you enter the lobby, a large fireplace crowned by a ceiling-high Chippendale mantel is the focal point. The elegantly tall windows, English style upholstered down cushioned sofas, red velvet side chairs,

Williamsburg blue painted walls, and crystal and bronze sconces reflect an era of opulence. In fact the mood throughout the inn is an alliance of gild and romance. The guest rooms reflect Old World elegance and charm in using lush draperies, half-canopied beds, marble-top dressers, and French chaises. Jacuzzis in the round add to the drama. A Bang and Olafson stereo system is employed in each room. Pampering guests is a tradition here, so complimentary California wines, aged bourbon, and French embroidered hankies in the bridal suites are caring reminders of that. Guests are often amused by the ceramic feline statues that are poised atop the satin bedcovers.

There are three fine dining rooms at the Lowell Inn. Each reflects the personality and vision of a member of the Palmer family. Conceived by Nelle, the George Washington Room combines the best elements of colonial fineries such as linen-covered tables set with English china and Sheffield silver. The waitresses are outfitted in crisp, Swiss embroidered organdy dresses. In the Garden Room you'll find a trout pond attributed to Art Sr., who, instead of fighting the elements of nature, brought the outdoors inside when an underground spring continued to seep through. An inspiration of Art Jr., and of international reputation, is the Matterhorn Room. In homage to his heritage, the crafts of the Swiss woodcarver were employed to recreate a memorable experience in the Swiss Alps when camaraderie, fondue, and wine made an everlasting impression upon Art and his companions.

Some of the prestigious awards received by the inn have been the Ivy Award in 1984 (Restaurant "Hall of Fame") and the Holiday Award for thirty years.

~~~~~~~~~~~~~~~~
THE FACTS

THE LOWELL INN
102 N. Second St., Stillwater, MN 55082. (612) 439-1100.
Innkeepers: Maureen and Arthur Palmer. Established in 1930. Open year round.
Rooms: 16 plus 5 suites. Bath: All pvt; 4 with Jacuzzis
Cost: $109–$189 high season, $89–$179 low season for All European Plan (no meals). $209–$289 high season, $189–$279 low season for All American Plan (Dinner and Breakfast). All major credit cards/cash/personal checks.
Limited smoking. AC. Children welcome. No pets.
Directions from Twin Cities: Take Hwy 36 east to downtown Stillwater, then a left turn onto Myrtle St. and a right onto 2nd St. Parking lot adjacent to Inn.

~~~~~~
THE OUTING LODGE AT PINE POINT
Manor Style in the Pines

Most people are surprised as they make their way down the driveway that encircles a lovely garden in front of this red brick European manor style lodge. Actually, its not-so-elegant beginnings were as a county poor farm in 1858. Later, in the 1920s, it served as a county nursing home.

When it had been abandoned for more than a decade, proprietor Lee Gohlike saw its potential and purchased it in 1983. A brilliant restoration, complete with five grand fireplaces, library, spacious dining room, eight guest suites, and an off-site three bedroom cottage, has been accomplished. Many of the antiques and artifacts have come from Lee Gohlike's collection; he has traveled extensively as an international auto broker. An example is the massive fireplace in the common reception area of the main floor that has been reassembled after travelling from Argentina. The honey-colored wide planked floors came from Minneapolis.

Five of the main lodge guest suites have whirlpool tubs, and four have sitting rooms. Each suite has a private bath.

A continental style breakfast is served in the common dining area overlooking a pine forest.

During the weekdays the lodge is exclusively open as an executive retreat and conference center. They also cater to wedding parties and give individualized service to brides. Beth Hillman, the planning manager, is very accommodating and related that the lodge's policy is "one of service oriented with a sense of community."

The lodge has also been acclaimed for its culinary events, which occur monthly and include such repasts as "Babette's Feast," a lavish seven-course meal with accompanying wines and cognac.

For your natural pleasure, the six acres belonging to the lodge and a surrounding 350-acre park are filled with well-groomed trails for cross-country skiing in winter and are popular with equestrians and hikers in the warmer months.

~~~~~~~~~~~~~~~~

THE FACTS

The Outing Lodge at Pine Point

11661 Myeron Road N., Stillwater, MN 55082. (612) 439-9747. Proprietor: Lee Gohlike. General Mgr: Jennifer Luhrs. Established 1988. Open year round on weekends as bed and breakfast.

Rooms: 8 suites, plus 1 cottage with 3 bedrooms

Baths: 8 pvt., 5 with whirlpool tubs. Cottage has shared bathroom.

Cost: $75 single. $100–125 double for suites.

$20 for each add'l person. MC/Visa/personal check.

Smoking in designated areas. Handicap accessible and one barrier-free suite. AC. Inquire about children. No pets.

Directions from Twin Cities: Take Hwy 36 east to County Rd. 15 in Stillwater. Go north on 15 for 3 miles to Hwy 96. Turn right; go 1.8 miles to County Rd. 55 and turn left. Go 1.7 miles and turn left again onto Myeron Rd. Go 1.2 miles to Outing Lodge driveway on the right.

~~~~~~

RIVERTOWN INN
Oldest B & B in Stillwater

This former mansion home of lumber baron John O'Brien was constructed in 1892. It was originally called "Alta Vista" because of its location overlooking the town of Stillwater and the scenic St. Croix. After undergoing renovation and restoration using original woodwork and chandeliers stored in the basement, this three-story Victorian lady, with its sweeping veranda that nearly encircles the house, was opened as Stillwater's first bed and breakfast, that was 1982. Some years later, in 1987, the present innkeepers and owners, Chuck and Judy Doughtery, found, quite by accident, that the Rivertown Inn was for sale. Degreed in hospitality management and working at the time as a regional manager of several restaurants in Michigan, Chuck decided to come and take a look. After twenty-four hours, the Doughertys had become the new owners.

Presently, you can choose from nine well-appointed rooms decorated with fine furnishings and antiques, each with its own bath. Some also have whirlpools, fireplaces, or woodburning stoves. The most romantic of these, Faith's Room, is a lovely chamber with an immense antique, walnut half-tester bed with canopy dressed in a delicate fine lace. The lovely marble-top dresser and fireplace add to the charm of the space, which has its own sitting area. A private whirlpool bath completes the set of amenities this room has to offer. Equally charming for those on a budget is Jessica's Room. With direct access to the second floor porch, which overlooks the St. Croix River, you can have sweet dreams in a beautiful brass bed and a soak in the old claw-foot tub in the bath off the hallway. Robes are provided for each guest when baths are not in the room.

Breakfast is served from a buffet in the spacious dining room and, in fine weather, on the main level porch. Since both Judy and Chuck have experience in the food and restaurant business, the breakfast buffet contains more than a dozen items, all prepared at the inn by your hosts. Some of these savories might include fruit-topped flan, cinnamon and caramel cakes, blueberry-glazed coffee cakes, and so on. There is a less elaborate spread on weekdays, but the same quality is provided.

Each of the three floors has a common sitting room for guests' convenience. When the house is nearly full, the Dougherty's arrange for a social hour, at which time tasty snacks, wine, or other beverages are served.

Other services available include tours of the inn by appointment; and lunch, supper, or afternoon teas can be arranged with the inn. Your hosts will also help you with other arrangements, such as scheduling excursions.

~~~~~~~~~~~~~~~~

THE FACTS

THE RIVERTOWN INN

306 W. Olive St., Stillwater, MN 55082. (612) 430-2955.

Innkeepers: Chuck & Judy Dougherty. Open year round. Established in 1982.

Rooms: 9 (1 on first floor). Baths: 9 pvt. (5 rooms have whirlpool tubs).

Cost: $49–$149/double. MC/Visa/Amex/personal check.

Smoke free. AC. Inquire about children.

Directions from Twin Cities: Hwy 36 east to Stillwater, then go to S. 3rd st. From 3rd St. turn left onto W. Olive. From I-94: Take MN Hwy 95 north to Stillwater.

~~~~~~

THE WILLIAM SAUNTRY MANSION*
Elegant Victorian Restoration with No Expense Spared

Guests must surely get the feeling that they are returning to another time as they enter the William Sauntry Mansion. Duane and Martha Hubbs, preservation activists for many years, purchased this late Victorian era mansion in Stillwater in 1988. With twenty years of restoration experience on twenty-five properties, they have gloriously restored the eccentric Sauntry's old mansion. Combining their talents, as no contractors were employed, the couple have provided a gracious in-town bed and breakfast. No detail is too insignificant, no decoration too extravagant, for this ambitious showcase restoration.

Sauntry, an entrepreneur whose wealth was reported to be over two million dollars at one time, lived here with his family in high style. This twenty-five room mansion was at one time connected to the "Gymnasium," a building Sauntry had constructed in the Moorish style, which housed a ballroom and swimming pool. An impressive collection of fine antiques and accessories add to the quality of the home with its beautiful stained glass windows, canvas painted ceiling, inlaid hardwood floors, and gracefully carved fireplaces. Your hosts take delight when you notice some detail of particular interest and are willing to offer further bits of knowledge.

The five guest rooms, all with hardwood floors, private baths, and many with fireplaces, were inspired by the family members of the Sauntry household. Joseph's Room, with its black and rose wallpaper and Renaissance revival bed appeals to romantics. William's Room, named for the master of the house, pays him tribute with an extraordinary German antique king-size bed with stained glass headboard. Across the hall is Mrs. LaFuegy's (Sauntry's mother-in-law) Room. Walls painted a cinnamon spice and, a unique black-enameled four-poster iron bed draped in shimmering satin invokes a mood of drama. Beltram, only son of Eunice and William, is the name applied to a lovely room papered in cabbage roses on a mint background. It provides one with a traditional bath, fireplace, and high-back oak bed. The demure Eunice, wife to William, is the name given to the room at the head of the stairs. With corner fireplace and a brass and iron bed serenely decorated, the room evokes a gentle charm.

Guests are pampered with wine and treats, plush terry robes, bubble baths, and chocolates at bedside.

Breakfast is served in the formal dining room on a cherry wood banquet table set in a grand style. Guests are treated to the gourmet cooking talents of both Duane and Martha as you savor a four-course Victorian style breakfast.

Enjoy the ambience of the downstairs parlors and music room, whose main feature is the Chickering grand piano. A painted canvas ceiling invoking the French Aubosson style in the formal parlor is an original feature of this home and has miraculously survived the many changes to the house.

~~~~~~~~~~~~

THE FACTS

WILLIAM SAUNTRY MANSION
626 N. Fourth St., Stillwater, MN 55082. (612) 430-2653.
Innkeepers: Duane and Martha Hubbs. Established in 1990. Open year round.
Rooms: 5, some with fireplaces   Baths: 5 pvt.
Cost: $89–$119. Midweek rates available. MC/Visa/Amex/cash/personal checks.
Smoke free. No children or pets.
Directions from Twin Cities: Take Hwy 36 east to downtown Stillwater. Take a left turn on Main and Myrtle Sts. Take Myrtle to N. 4th St. and turn right. Mansion is on the corner of Maple and N. 4th St.

*National Register of Historic Places

~~~~~~

SHADY RIDGE FARM BED AND BREAKFAST
The Lady Loves Her Llamas

Sheila Fugina, after retiring as a journalist, says she wanted to stay at home and mend fences. So she and her husband Britt purchased the old Schaefer farm in Houlton, Wisconsin, with its 1890 red brick farmhouse. They spent one-and-a-half years renovating it and making it inviting to guests. To add to the attraction, Sheila decided she wanted to raise llamas, so they purchased their first two in 1988 and fell in love with the gentle beasts. They were everything the couple had hoped they would be and even more. Soon after, they acquired Lindsay, an expectant llama who added to their small herd. Sheila loves to talk about llamas and encourages her guests to become involved with them either by having a photo taken with them or by taking a llama on a picnic complete with sacks packed with breakfasts prepared by Sheila.

Apart from the llamas, this lovely country inn set on rolling hills offers beautiful scenery, woodlands, and orchards for hiking, cross-country skiing, or bird-watching.

Breakfast is served either in the dining room or on the sun porch and even in your bed upon special request. Sheila is proud to state that the jams and jellies are made from fruits raised on Shady Ridge. She also incorporates into her egg dishes the vegetables grown organically on the farm.

Each of the three guest rooms bears a family member's name, and uniquely features mementos and memorabilia of that person. Sheila has created an enchanted atmosphere of comfort and intimacy. For instance, Maize's Room, named for Sheila's grandmother, is painted in a soft, pale yellow stenciled with a border of roses. This room displays a photo montage, and a comfortable antique wrought iron bed dressed with a brightly colored quilt. It shares a bath with Catherine's room. Twin beds in Catherine's room have oak headboards fashioned from old bookcases that are filled with memorabilia from Britt's childhood in Korea. There are handhooked rugs with fanciful designs, colorful quilts, and a tin ceiling. The largest guest room is named for Oliver, Sheila's father. It features a queensize, four-poster bed and private bath. It is handsomely decorated with a red and green stenciled border and antique furnishings.

Guests also enjoy the main parlor on wintery nights, when they can play the old pump organ or engage in such old-fashioned parlor games as cribbage. In all, Sheila seems to have a full life as innkeeper and breeder of llamas, much more than as a mender of fences.

~~~~~~~~~~~~~~~~
THE FACTS
SHADY RIDGE FARM BED & BREAKFAST
410 Highland View Rd., Houlton, WI 54082 (715) 549-6258. Innkeepers: Sheila and Britt Fugina. Open year round. Established in 1990.
Rooms: 3
Baths: 1 pvt., 1 shared
Cost: $55–$75 double. Cash/personal check.
Smoke free. Inquire about children. Ceiling fans.
Directions from Twin Cities: Take I-94 east to Hudson. Take Hwy 35 north to County E and then take E east 4 miles. Shady Ridge Farm is on the left.
~~~~~~

THE ASA PARKER HOUSE
Enduring Elegance in This Historic Inn

Resident innkeeper Marjorie Bush has found a winning formula. Antique-filled rooms, English fabrics and wallcoverings, goose down comforters, and extravagant breakfasts in this graciously restored historic home all add up to a successful bed and breakfast. Marjorie's years of experience as an innkeeper and her travel abroad have contributed to such success. In addition, her many talents are expressed at the Asa Parker House, primarily as a gourmet cook. Original entrées such as wild rice n' bacon casserole and grand-marnier-stuffed french toast have received prestigious awards. Dried florals are another area of expression at which she has attained success, as the four-star St. Paul Hotel has often used her arrangements throughout the hotel.

In 1986 Marjorie purchased the Asa Parker House in Marine on the Croix, Minnesota. It was originally the home built in 1856 for one of the founding members of the first lumber company in Minnesota. Sitting on a knoll overlooking the St. Croix Valley, the elegant lines of this Greek Revival structure always capture your eye as you pass by.

There are three guest rooms and one suite. A favorite of many celebrants is the Alice O'Brien Room, a very private suite of three rooms. A comfortable queensize bed is tucked under the eaves, and a bath chamber with whirlpool is in adjacent quarters. There is also a lovely wicker-filled sitting room as part of this suite. Another favorite, because of its lovely views of the valley, is the Isabella Parker Room. A bright and sun-filled room, it contains an antique white enameled bed dressed in English florals. You step up to a white-tiled private bath with claw-footed tub attached to this room.

Early morning baskets containing tea and coffee arrive at your door each day. Breakfast is a grand affair here, as guests gather around the perfectly set tables in the dining room. Eggs Wellington with crab and basil sauce or another of Marjorie's award-winning entrées might be the fare. Fresh fruit, juice, and other beverages are also served.

Afternoon tea with sweets is served on weekdays, and on weekends a proper afternoon tea is served with sandwiches, scones, and sweets.

For additional pleasures, stroll in the gardens, play a game of lawn croquet, or try tennis at the court. In wintertime, cross-country skiers enjoy this location as right out the door you are on groomed trails.

~~~~~~~~~~~~~~~~

THE FACTS

THE ASA PARKER HOUSE
17500 St. Croix Trail No., Marine on the Croix, MN 55047.
(612) 433-5248.
Innkeeper: Marjorie Bush. Established 1986. Open year round.
Rooms: 3 plus 1 suite. Baths: 4, all pvt., 1 with whirlpool tub
Cost: $99–$135 double. Midweek $79–$105. Inquire about business and corporate rates. MC/Visa/cash/personal checks.
Smoke free. AC. No children or pets.
Directions from Twin Cities: Take Hwy 36 east to Hwy 95 north. Go 10 miles past Stillwater to Marine. Take a left turn onto Co. Rd. 4. Go a half a block and make a sharp right onto 5th St.; follow 5th St. for one long block to sign for Asa Parker parking.

~~~~~~

PLEASANT LAKE COUNTRY INN
Pleasant Memories from the Past

Pleasant memories from the past provide pleasing memories for the present at this secluded country inn, standing on the shores of Lake Pleasant, just outside of Osceola. Bonfires at night gather guests and family members for storytelling or other affable exchange. Your hosts,

Charlene and Richard Berg, tell stories with their contemporary country home in which they have preserved bits of memorabilia from family history, dating back to 1855 when the Berg homesteaders started a dairy farm. A herd of forty-eight Holsteins graze the pastures, and guests are invited to view the activities at the dairy barn.

Guest rooms honoring their "grands" contain carefully arranged favorite things and lovingly displayed ancestral family photos. Spacious rooms with views of the lake, queensize beds, and private bathrooms (some with whirlpools) make you comfortable during your stay.

Breakfast is served with the family, and Charlene enjoys preparing honey puff pancakes and honey-baked french toast, and serving honey obtained from her own beehives.

Breads are made on the premises. It's teamwork here! Charlene grists the wheat kernels and prepares the stoneground flour while Richard does the baking.

They say you can hear the fish jumping in summertime at Pleasant Lake. Memories are made of this, and for a bit more pleasure, the Bergs send you home with your own special loaf of their baked goods.

~~~~~~~~~~~~~~~~

THE FACTS

PLEASANT LAKE INN,
2238 60th Ave. Osceola, WI 54020. (715) 294-2545.
Innkeepers: Charlene and Richard Berg. Established 1990. Open year round.
Rooms: 3   Baths: 3 pvt., 2 with whirlpool tubs
Cost: $70–$90 double. Midweek and multiple-night discounts available. Business rate $40 single. MC/Visa/cash/personal or traveler's checks.
Smoke free. AC. Children welcome. No pets.
Directions from Twin Cities: Take I-94 east to Hudson, WI. Exit to WI Hwy 35 north to Osceola. Right on County M; go 2.5 miles to 240th St., right turn; go 1 mile to 60th Ave., left turn, 1.5 miles to Pleasant Lake Inn.

~~~~~~

ST. CROIX RIVER INN-BED & BREAKFAST
Romantic Interlude on the River

Designed as a soothing environment with outstanding views of the river, the St. Croix River Inn accomplishes just that as you enter the main lobby and pass through to the deck overlooking the river. Robert Marshall and a group of investors purchased this 1908 Dutch colonial style stone house in 1984 and soon thereafter developed this charming inn. Originally the home was owned by C. W. Staples and remained in that family until Mr. Marshall purchased it. Osceola saw three generations of Staples as druggists from 1873 to 1939.

Seven very private suites are classically decorated with reproductions of eighteenth-century antiques, attractive window dressings, and plush carpeting. At one time Osceola had a thriving steamboat manufacturing business, and there have been ten known steamboats built there. In tribute to this history, the seven suites take their names from these old steamboats. Featuring an enclosed four-season porch and deck, the G. B. Knapp Suite, a spacious room with four-poster bed, gas fireplace, and Jacuzzi with views of the river is one of my favorites. Probably the most romantic is the Jennie Hays Suite on the second floor. The drama of a Palladian window set in a high vaulted ceiling adds to the magnificent views seen from this room. Enhancing the beauty and mood of the room are the elegant four-poster bed and gas fireplace. All of the suites have private bathrooms and whirlpool tubs.

The Osceola Suite on the lower level can accommodate small business meetings and has a full kitchen. A game room on the upper level is papered in a riverboat scene and is a common area for guests.

Since there is a nonresident innkeeper, arrangements need to be made to leave the keys to your room at an appointed time for you to let yourself in. Snacks and beverages are left on the buffet in the main lobby for guests to enjoy at their convenience. Wine is complimentary to all suites. Other amenities include terry robes, TV's, and stereo music provided to each suite.

Breakfast is served in your room, and the menu alternates every other day. Homemade muffins, coffee cakes with either banana french toast served with warm maple syrup or ham and cheese omelette is the entrée. Also included for you to enjoy are fruits, juice and other choice of beverages. All is served at your bedside.

If you are looking for a romantic interlude with privacy near the top of your list, and if you don't mind the prices, you can be sure to find it at the St. Croix River Inn.

~~~~~~~~~~~~~~~~
THE FACTS

ST. CROIX RIVER INN
305 River St., Osceola, WI 54020. (715) 294-4248.
Innkeeper: Bev Johnson. Established in 1984. Open year round.
Rooms: 7 suites, some with fireplaces. Baths: 7 pvt., all with whirlpools.
Cost: $125–$200/dbl, weekends. $85–$125/dbl, midweek. MC/Visa
Amex/cash/checks. Business persons receive special discounts during midweek.
Limited smoking. AC. Children welcome. No pets.
Directions from Twin Cities: Take Hwy 36 east to Hwy 95 north, then Hwy 243 east to Osceola. At first stop sign turn left. Go north to 3rd Ave. and then left to River St.

~~~~~~

NOTES

NOTES

*Cover Park Manor,
Oak Park Heights.
Left, Molly Jean's
Room.*

Adell's Suite. It has an adjoining room and bath chambers.

The Ann Bean House - The Guest Room.

The grand stairway and foyer.

Cynthia's Room in the east tower.

The Tower Room, a suite with breakfast nook tucked in the tower.

Battle Hollow Bed & Breakfast of Stillwater.

The elegant music room.

Ella's Room has a fireplace and gracefully curved iron bed.

The elegant
mid-Victorian
dining room of
the Brunswick Inn
in Stillwater.

Miss Anna's Room, a guest suite at the inn.

The sunroom which adjoins the Cadiz Suite.

The Elephant Walk of Stillwater.

The Raffles Room.

A display of oriental object d'art in the double parlor.

The Heirloom Inn - one of the oldest Bed and Breakfasts in Stillwater.

Fine antique furnishings in the double parlor.

One of the comfortable and well appointed guest rooms.

James A. Mulvey Residence Inn, Stillwater.

Pictured is the Grueby fireplace, one of two known in Minnesota.

The elegant Moorcroft Room with its canopied tester bed.

The Laurel Street Inn, Stillwater, MN.

The Murdock Suite. Named for the man who built the house in 1857.

The main parlor of the inn has access to the porch overlooking the St. Croix.

The historic Lowell Inn of Stillwater.

Dressed in Swiss-embroidered frocks the lovely waitresses of the George Washington Room are ready to serve you. The tables are dressed in fine linens and set with Spode china.

The Outing Lodge at Pine Point, Stillwater.

Left. Dark green marble tiles add to the luxury of this guest suite with whirlpool tub and antique bed.

The Rivertown Inn. Stillwater's oldest Bed & Breakfast.

Faith's Room with high walnut canopy bed.

Julie's Room. A bright, cheerful room has an antique walnut bed and view of the river.

Music parlor of the Sauntry Mansion.

The William Sauntry Mansion and side gardens, Stillwater.

Bentwood screen in Mooris design.

William's Room with its extraordinary antique German bed.

Shady Ridge Farm Bed & Breakfast in Houlton, WI.

Oliver's Room with its colorful quilt.

Innkeeper, Sheila Fugina, with one of her llama friends.

Innkeeper, Majorie Bush. Double parlors of Asa Parker House, Marine.

The Asa Parker House with its elegant lines captures your eye.

The Isabella Parker Room.   *The table is set for breakfast.*

The Berg's of Pleasant Lake Inn, Osceola, as they prepare their homebaked loaves of bread.

Joseph's Room. French doors open onto your own private sun-porch which overlooks the lake.

e St. Croix River Inn, Osceola.

Jennie Hays Room with its high vaulted ceiling.

Taylors Falls Princess as it makes its way down the St. Croix River.

The Great Hearth. Forgotten Tymes, Siren.

Historical Outlines and Points of Interest

TAYLORS FALLS, MN

In the summer of 1838 Jesse Taylor and his associate Benjamin Baker arrived from Fort Snelling, MN on the west bank of the St. Croix River at the head of steamboat navigation. Soon they constructed a mill complex (The Baker's Fall Mill Company) which marked the beginning of the first permanent settlement and named it "Taylor's Place" and the lower falls "Bakers' Falls" (the falls or rapids extend upstream several miles from the present bridge at Hwy 8, and are mostly hidden by the NSP power dam and flowage). Mr. Baker died and Mr. Taylor eventually moved to Stillwater, later selling his claim to Joshua Taylor (not a relative) in 1846. Soon after 1850, new settlers were arriving at an increasing rate, one of whom was W.H.C. Folsom, who constructed the first frame business building of the town. In 1851 Taylors Falls was officially designated in memory of Jesse Taylor. In 1856 the first bridge to span the St. Croix River was constructed between Taylors Falls and St. Croix Falls, WI. Today, Taylors Falls is the site of many historic buildings and is full of diverse recreational opportunities.

Points of Interest—

Angel Hill Historic District - Sitting under the spire of the United Methodist Church, Angel Hill is a collection of nineteenth century buildings of classic Greek Revival architecture. The entire area is on the National Register of Historic Places. Check with the Chamber of Commerce to find out about home tours. (612) 465-6661.

Interstate Park - 295 acres adjacent to the wild and scenic St. Croix River. Site of the world famous Glacial Garden containing more than 200 potholes. There are forty-eight riverside campsites, hiking trails, rock climbing, canoe rentals, tour boats, picnic shelters, visitor center and museum. (612) 465-5711

Wild River State Park - Wild River is located just north of Taylors Falls off Hwy 95 and includes 7000 acres and eighteen miles frontage along the St. Croix River. Semi-modern campsites are available year round. Thirty-five mile trail for hiking, horseback riding and cross country skiing. An all season trail center, picnic shelter and interpretive center with twelve month naturalist programming are also available. (612) 583-2125

W.H.C. Folsom House - Located on Government Road in the Angel Hill District, the house possesses an imposing view of the river valley. Completed in 1856 by W.H.C. Folsom, the main house reflects both the Greek and Federal style popular with many New England settlers who came to this area. Open daily with guided tours from Memorial Day weekend to October 15 (1:00 to 4:30 p.m.). Group tours at other hours or in closed season by advance reservation. Historical Society, Taylors Falls, Mn. 55084. (612) 465-3125, 465-4435 or 465-7695.

ST. CROIX FALLS, WI

Although Marine had the first operating sawmill in the Valley, a group of eight adventurous men (Franklin Steele, Jeremiah Russell, George Fitch, Samuel Stambaugh, John S. McInnes, Dr. John Emerson, Daniel P. Bushnell and Norman Kittson) made claim to the Valley's earliest settlement at St. Croix Falls. They formed what was to be called the St. Croix Lumber Co. and began constructing a sawmill in 1837. From the beginning the lumber company was plagued by problems of organization and location. This was a more rugged site and the group "experienced great difficulties in building a dam and log boom. In fact, not until 1841 was the mill ready to saw its first timber....", so wrote James T. Dunn in his book, The St. Croix Midwest Border River. Actually, the story of St. Croix Falls' early years is a drama fought in the courts for decades over rightful ownership of the St. Croix Lumber Co. This impeded the progress of the town and it was not until 1874 that J. Stannard Baker came to St. Croix Falls and with competent management in real estate was responsible for the development of the Falls area. However, dreams of harvesting power from the Falls was never realized until 1906 when the Minneapolis General Electric Company constructed a dam supplying Minneapolis with its first electricity brought from outside the city. Today Northern States Power Company owns the facility that generates power to the surrounding area. A twin village to Taylors Falls, St. Croix Falls shares the natural and scenic beauty of the river at this point where the river becomes more slow moving and the bluffs rise high.

Points of Interest—
National Park Service Visitor Center and Museum - Information regarding the riverway and museum collection of wildlife and fauna of the area may be viewed here. (715) 483-3284.

Wisconsin Interstate Park and Interpretive Center - Camping, picnicking, swimming beach, hiking, and cross-country ski trails. (715) 483-3747.

NORTH BRANCH, MN
It was first known as "The Branch" or North Branch Station, named for the north branch of the Sunrise River, which is a branch of the St. Croix. Originally an aspiring settlement on the Lake Superior and Mississippi Railroad line between the Twin Cities and Duluth, it was platted by the Western Land Association, a land-holding affiliate of the railroad. After the Civil War the area was settled by "Yankees" and later an influx of "Swedes". It became a post office and station in 1870 and was incorporated in 1881. Also known as a profitable potato growing region. Today it has become a desirable location with proximity to the Twin Cities.

Points of Interest—
Vande Kamp Auctioneering - Col. L. "Bob" Vande Kamp, Jr., Auctioneer. Vacationers Welcome! If you have never been to an auction, join the Colonel for fun and excitement. Auctions are held year round. Please call for auction dates and locations. (612) 583-3121.

LINDSTROM, SHAFER AND FRANCONIA

Swedish immigrant Daniel Lindstrom arrived in America in 1853 from Hassel, Sweden. The following year he purchased some 134 acres of land in the town that bears his name, Lindstrom. On the site where the Dinnerbel Restaurant is now located, he erected a farm. Later he built a home which still stands on Lake Blvd. The city, which originally included all of Lindstrom's farm and an additional forty acres is located in the Chisago Lakes area (included are Chisago City, and Center City). Characterized by placid lakes and gently rolling farmlands (Shafer) this region was almost exclusively settled by Swedish immigrants. Hidden away on the banks of the St. Croix River is what remains of the city of Franconia. When the early settlers traveled up the river, Franconia had become one of the main entry points. Remaining on the banks of the river are but a few fine homes reminiscent of those times. Swedish playwright and author, Vilhelm Moberg came to the area in 1948 to do research for what became a trilogy of books on Swedish immigration (The Emigrants, Unto a Good Land, The Settlers and Last Letter Home). A popular movie, The Emigrants, which was later serialized for television, was based on these works. In 1990 the State of Minnesota dedicated The Moberg Trail. The trail traces the remnants of the major route used by the first Swedish settlers. It runs from Taylors Falls to Forest Lake, Minnesota.

Points of Interest—

Amador Heritage Center - History museum of central Chisago County. Constructed in the early 1900's as a school and now houses the history center. Open Sunday afternoon between 1:00 p.m. and 5:00 p.m. Located just off Hwy 95 in Almelund, Minnesota.

Karl and Kristina Oscar - a statue erected to the memory of the Swedish spirit of fictionalized characters, Karl and Kristina, which Moberg used in his trilogy. Lake Blvd., Lindstrom, MN.

Center City Historic District - Includes some of the fine homes of Summit Avenue and the Chisago Lake Swedish Evangelical Lutheran Church, which is the second oldest Lutheran church site in Minnesota.

Chisago County Guide and Tourism Service. Historical tours of the area. Reservations required. (612) 257-1579.

HINCKLEY, MN

September 1, 1894 marked an infamous day in the history of the railroad town of Hinckley, Minnesota and surrounding communities. One of the worst fires in this nation's history proved catastrophic for 400 people as they perished in this disaster. Such an indelible memory on the community of this event served as impetus to erect a museum which tells the tales of many who survived (see below). Hinckley recovered and became a prosperous agricultural and industrial city. Popular because of its location about half-way between Duluth, MN and the Twin Cities.

Points of Interest—
Hinckley Fire Museum - Exhibits on the events of the Great Hinckley Fire of 1894. Located in the St. Paul and Duluth Railroad Depot, which is on the National Register of Historic Places. Open May through October, 10 a.m. to 5 p.m. 106 Old Hwy 61. (612) 384-7338.

St. Croix State Park - Scenic bluffs, rolling hills, groomed trails. Camping, hiking, biking and cross-country skiing with a river view. Located on Hwy 48 East of Hinckley. (612) 384-6591.

Moose Lake-Hinckley Fire Trail - A thirty six and a half mile, paved blacktop bike trail surrounded by forests of pine and aspen. In Hinckley go west to Old Hwy 61, turn north and continue to Co. Rd. 18, turn west across tracks to parking lot with facilities on the Grindstone River. You can access at Finlayson also.

FINLAYSON, MN
This community largely developed due to the efforts of John Oldenberg, a Finnish immigrant who purchased lands for the development of the railroad when establishing the line between St. Paul and Duluth. Today it remains a farming community with a population of around 300 and is the site of the Pine County Historical Museum.

BALSAM LAKE, WI
The peaceful village of about 800 people is located in one of the oldest resort areas in the northwest, situated on the Balsam Lake. The lake has sixty five miles of shoreline and is popular for sailboats, speed boats, canoes and water skiers. A tidy Main Street has a real old-fashioned soda fountain and a museum which has exhibits detailing the town's history of logging and immigration. A diversity of ethnic groups settled in this area; Danish, Swedish, Norwegian, German, Irish and Scottish all claim heritage.

Points of Interest—
Polk County Museum - Built in 1899 and is listed on the National Register of Historic Places. Three floors of exhibits with over fifty galleries. One block south is the Polk County Rural Life Museum which is also worth a visit. Both museums are open Memorial Day through Labor Day. Weekdays and Sundays 12:30-4:00 p.m. and Saturdays and Holidays 10:00-4:00 p.m. (715) 485-3136.

FREDERIC, WI
When passing through Frederic on the Wisconsin State Hwy 35 one notices its prettiness. Broad streets lead through this tidy community set in gently rolling hills. The village comprises attractive homes and buildings mostly constructed around the turn of the century. In its heyday, around 1901, this was a bustling logging town. Presently, Frederic has established a firm economic base in farming, industry and tourism.

Points of Interest—
Gandy Dancer Trail - Purchased from the railroad for the purpose of a multi-use trail, the Gandy Dancer begins in Polk County, Wisconsin. You are just a few hundred feet to an entry point from the Gandy Dancer Bed and Breakfast. When completed, this trail will meander through northwestern Wisconsin, cross the St. Croix River into Minnesota, and then trail back into Wisconsin.

BURNETT AND WASHBURN COUNTIES
(includes Danbury, Lewis, Siren and Springbrook, Wisconsin)
It is important to remember that the Ojibwe Indians were the primary inhabitants of this land, living well from its resources of wild game, fish, berries, maple sugar and wild rice. Neither can we minimize the British and French fur trade society in which Indian and voyageur developed a kind of cultural exchange, sharing customs and knowledge in an orderly fashion. Reflecting this history are two important sites: Fort Folle Avoine (on the Yellow River) near Danbury replicates a fur trading post of the early nineteenth century and is open to the public. The other is the Band of St. Croix Ojibwe Indian Reservations, one located west of Hertel, Wisconsin and one just southeast of Danbury, Wisconsin. These reservations were created to lay lands aside for the Indians after the Treaty of 1837, whereby the Indians sold most of their lands to the white government. After which, this northwestern part of Wisconsin was opened to settlement from European immigration and Yankee entrepreneurial endeavors. Lumbering and later some farming were the primary industries. Today, these counties are chiefly supported through tourism, resort communities and vacation homes.

Points of Interest—
Forts Folle Avoine - Historical site recreating a fur trading post of the early nineteenth century operated by the North West Company Fur Post. Four miles north of Webster, Wisconsin on Hwy 35. (715) 866-8890 or (715) 349-2219.

Crex Meadows Wildlife Area - encompasses over 30,000 acres. Except for 2,399 acres of refuge, the entire area is open to public hunting and trapping. Wetlands have been restored and maintained as an excellent habitat for waterfowl and furbearers. Project headquarters on site. Located one-half mile north of the village of Grantsburg, Wisconsin and is accessible via Wisconsin State Hwys 70, 48 and 87.

AMBERWOOD BED & BREAKFAST
Home in Family since Turn of the Century

Because it is ablaze each autumn with the golden browns and crimson of the many maples surrounding the main house, Amberwood is an appropriate name for this seven-acre country estate near St. Croix Falls, Wisconsin. Donna Dombrock proudly tells us that this 1880's Italianate style home has been in her family since the turn of the century.

Creatively decorated in found and reclaimed objects and original art work, Donna achieves an ambience of distinction. Grandpa's rocker, rich oak woods, and attractive draperies make up a handsome dining room.

Each guest room on the second floor is named for one of Donna's sisters, each contributing paintings or handmade objects to the rooms. Painted in what I called a Victorian rose, accented with burgundy, pale yellow and blues, Janet's Room contains a handsome queensize brass bed, turn-of-the-century oak dresser, and tidy table and chairs. Janet stitched the wonderful balloon curtains, dust ruffle, and quilt found on the bed. Nancy takes credit for the guest room with craftsman style oak bed, as she hand crocheted the window toppers and handloomed the floor mats. Diane's Room is rustic country all the way, from the charming window shutters to the uncommon ironwood Adirondack double-size bed covered in Grandmother's Flower Garden quilt. There are two bathrooms on the second floor, one of which is shared and the other private. When only two guest rooms are rented, each has its own bathroom.

Breakfast, which is always a full fare, is served in the dining room, on the front porch, or in your room. Donna is very health conscious, so she believes in serving low fat egg dishes with vegetables, and homemade whole grain breads and pancakes. Fresh fruit, hot or cold cereals, and yoghurt are always served.

Donna has taken care to provide an atmosphere of comfort and quiet. At your request, she will arrange for a masseuse or Tai Chi instruction on the premises while staying as a guest. Small groups are welcome for these special services.

~~~~~~~~~~~~~~~~
THE FACTS
AMBERWOOD BED AND BREAKFAST
320 McKenney St., St. Croix Falls, WI 54024. (715)483-9355.
Innkeeper: Donna Dombrock. Established in 1990. Open year round.
Rooms: 3   Baths: 1 shared, 1 pvt.
Cost: $60–$75 double. Cash/personal or traveler's checks.
Smoke free. Inquire about children. No pets.
Directions from Twin Cities: Take I-35 north to exit 132 to Hwy 8 east to St. Croix Falls, then Hwy 35 south about 1 mile to McKenney St. Turn right; it is 2nd house on the right.

COUNTRY BED & BREAKFAST
Tall Tales at This Traditional Country B & B

If ever you wish to meet a couple who fit your idea of bed and breakfast hosts, Lois and Bud Barott do that very well. Congenial, attentive, and entertaining, they make you feel a part of their family straightaway. Bud has a reputation for spinning tales, and you soon find this to be true. Lois relates that this, her girlhood home, has been in the family since 1938, when her dad purchased it from the Thorsander family who had lived there since the 1880s. Located near Shafer, Minnesota, this red brick farmhouse, with its white-pillared front porch, is apparently rare for these parts; it was built in 1869 by a Swedish immigrant family named Olson. It has always been a farm, and Lois and Bud retain thirty-eight acres.

Another interesting story is that Vilhelm Moberg, the Swedish author who researched early Swedish immigration to this area and wrote the book on which the movie "The Immigrants" was based, visited this home in 1948 shortly after Bud and Lois married. It appears he was instructed by a relative of Lois in Sweden to bear a wedding gift to the Shafer country home. Lois is proud of her Swedish heritage and honors Swedish water colorist Carl Larsson by naming the library for him. Several of his watercolors are displayed upon the walls as well as other Swedish handicrafts. The room, with a large mission sofa and antique library table, functions as a lounge for guests and is well supplied with games, books, and other reading material.

The home itself, with its wide painted pine plank floors, is furnished comfortably in country antiques and handmades. All three guest rooms are on the second floor. The Little Room contains an attractively decorated single bed and seems a cozy place to spend the night. Across the hall is the Lavender Suite, a bright, cheerful and serene room with antique double-size painted white iron bed crisply dressed in a quilt handmade by Lois. The print on the wall reflects memories from her childhood as she, her mother, and sister were reading stories in this very room. These two rooms share a bath down the hall. Country Estates has its own private bath with old fashioned claw-foot tub for soaking, and an antique, double-size iron bed painted jade green. A soft floral rose wallpaper is the background.

Breakfast is served in the country kitchen near the woodburning stove, and this is where you gain the full benefit of country hospitality. While Bud prepares his specialty omelettes, Lois flips the buttermilk pancakes served with their own maple syrup. Ham, bacon, and sausage also come along, as well as a fresh fruit bowl served with yoghurt and juice. To top it all off is Lois's own recipe for Swedish egg coffee.

After such a hearty breakfast you might want to try the hiking trails on site or nearby recreational opportunities on the St. Croix River.

Bud and Lois don't want to forget you after you've left their home, so they have been keeping a photo album of their guests for many years.

~~~~~~~~~~~~~~~~

THE FACTS

COUNTRY BED & BREAKFAST

32030 Ranch Trail, Shafer, MN 55074. (612) 257-4773.

Innkeepers: Bud and Lois Barott. Established in l982. Open year round.

Rooms: 3   Baths: 1 pvt., l shared.

Cost: $55 single, $95 double. Cash/personal checks.

Smoke free. AC. Children above 12 years welcome. No pets.

Directions: In MN take I-35 north to Hwy 8 exit. Go east to County Rd. 21 in Shafer. Go north on 21 to Ranch Trail. In WI, take Hwy 8 west to Shafer and follow County 21 north.

~~~~~~

THE OLD FRANCONIA HOTEL BED & BREAKFAST
Family Home Was Once a Hotel

Up the hill it came in 1890, from the flats of the riverbanks of the St. Croix, to its present site on Old Franconia Trail in Shafer, Minnesota. Once a hotel owned by Nils Bylander, this Italianate style structure was built to accommodate the needs of a small, prosperous logging town. When the town had its demise, Bylander moved it to the farmlands, where it has remained in the same family for more than a century. Today, it serves as a bed and breakfast under the caring attention of Cheryl and Dennis Smolik.

Enjoying its position among mature maple trees, this home provides a little bit of country not far off the beaten path. Discovering a flair for decoration and a keen eye for arranging she had been unaware of, Cheryl, a registered nurse, has masterfully pulled off a charming look to her guest rooms. Located on the second floor, the three guest rooms follow the seasons, moving from Vinter (winter) in great-grandma's spoon-carved bed; to Vår (spring), with its hand-stenciled ivy border on candlelit beige walls and Jenny Lind bed covered with a hand-crocheted bedcöver; to Höst (autumn), a room of quiet grace with its fine feather painted walls and handsome oak bed set. To show her Swedish heritage, Cheryl publishes the names of the rooms in the tongue of her ancestors. Two modern and comfortable bathrooms are shared by guests.

Breakfast is served on the round dining table in the large country kitchen in front of an expansive window. Gourmet coffees, sausage, and pancakes topped with maple syrup collected on this farm are served with fresh fruit and an orange Julius.

Maple syrup has been a family business for decades, and the Smoliks share this heritage with guests as a small jar of the lovely sweet syrup is tendered as a memento of your stay.

~~~~~~~~~~~~~~~~

THE FACTS

THE OLD FRANCONIA HOTEL BED AND BREAKFAST

19585 Franconia Trail, Shafer, MN 55074. (612) 257-0779.

Innkeepers: Dennis and Cheryl Smolik. Established in 1993. Open year round.

Rooms: 3   Baths: 1 pvt., 1 shared

Cost: $55 single, $65 double. Cash/personal or traveler's checks.
Smoke free. AC. Children welcome. No pets.
Directions from Twin Cities: Take I-35 north to exit 132 to Hwy 8. Take Hwy 8 east to Shafer. At junction of Hwy 95 and 8, turn right onto 95. Go .3 mile to Franconia Trail; turn right. House is 1st on left.

~~~~~~

THE COTTAGE
Impressive Views of the River Coupled with Privacy

An unexpected turn onto the road through the white gates of an old country estate near Taylors Falls, leads you to the green-stained cedar shake roof and crisp white-trimmed grey eighteenth-century style English country home, holding an envious position atop a bluff overlooking the St. Croix River. Many superlatives come to mind as one reflects on the bounty of this natural setting among stately oaks and unimpeded vistas. Larry Collins, a professor of Spanish literature, at a St. Paul university, and his soft-spoken wife, Eleanor, an art resource librarian, decided that their guest house needed restoration. So pleased with their accomplishments, they felt compelled to share this with others and opened their bed and breakfast in June 1991.

Architect William Channing Whitney designed this structure (he also designed St. Paul's governor's mansion) for George Lane, founder of the investment firm of Lane, Piper, and Jaffray (now Piper, Jaffray and Hopwood). It was built in 1929 and served as a summer home and retreat for Lane.

Through a breezeway you enter your own private retreat decorated in a European cottage style. The main level room is comfortable, informal, and inviting with a sofa, table, and two chairs. The dining table is set in "English Rose" Franciscan china. Hardwood oak floors and braided rugs enrich the room. The bedroom, located on the upper level, contains a queensize bed with upholstered headboard, and from the bedroom window a glance to the east will reward you with superb views of the river. The bathroom is modern with tub and shower.

Breakfast is served at your convenience as the refrigerator is stocked with beverages and breakfast items such as fresh fruit and cheeses. Breads, muffins, jams and jellies also accompany your meal.

Your hosts provide you with snacks and refreshments upon arrival, and then you are free to enjoy the grounds or explore the Taylors Falls area.

~~~~~~~~~~~~~~~~~~

THE FACTS
THE COTTAGE BED AND BREAKFAST
Box 71, Taylors Falls, MN 55084. (612) 465-3595.
Innkeepers: Larry and Eleanor Collins. Established 1991. Open Feb.- Dec.
Rooms: one, 2-room suite   Bath: 1 pvt.
Cost: $98 single/double. 2 or more nights $91.50 double. Midweek rates. MC/Visa/cash/personal checks.

Smoke free. No children or pets.

Directions from Twin Cities: I-35 north to exit 132 to Hwy 8. Take Hwy 8 east 20 miles to Herberg Rd. Left onto Herberg Rd., which is 1st left after intersection of 8 and 95. Take 1 mile to white gates. Follow road to The Cottage. From Wisconsin: Take Hwy 8 west to just before the intersection of Hwy 95 and Hwy 8.

~~~~~~

McLane House Bed & Breakfast
Informal Style on the Main Street

When immigrants and homesteaders came to Minnesota to purchase land they came to this building. Since Taylors Falls was deemed a central location, the government established a land office here. It served as such from 1863 to 1916; thereafter, it became residential.

Drawn by the recreational opportunities of the valley and the beauty of the St. Croix, Cindy McLane acquired this vintage building. Cindy travelled frequently on business and found herself enjoying many of the bed and breakfasts as an alternative to motels or hotels. She was thus motivated to found her own B & B.

An informal, homey decor and Cindy provide one with all the comforts of home: soft, comfortable sofas by the fireside, snacks before turning in for the night, and breakfast in Grandma's Gourmet Kitchen, where you can enjoy delicious orange cinnamon muffins prepared with Cindy's specialty preserves.

There are three guest rooms on the second floor and all share one large bath with tub and shower. The largest guest room, Cindy's Study, has a queensize bed, sitting area, and balcony with private entrance that brings you to the woods above.

A continental breakfast is served on weekdays, but Cindy outdoes herself on weekends with a full hearty breakfast of bacon, sausage, omelettes, waffles, fried potatoes, muffins, and wheat bread.

Check out Cindy's old book collection if you visit.

~~~~~~~~~~~~~~~~
THE FACTS
McLane House Bed and Breakfast
505 Bench Street, Taylors Falls, MN 55084. (612) 465-4832.
Innkeeper: Cindy McLane. Established 1989. Open year round.
Rooms: 3   Baths: 1 shared
$65–$75. Midweek discounts and multiple-night discounts. MC/Visa/cash/personal or traveler's checks.
Smoke free. Children 12 and older welcome. No pets.
Directions from Twin Cities: Take I-35 north to exit 132 to Hwy 8. Take to downtown Taylors Falls.

~~~~~~

THE OLD JAIL COMPANY*
Privacy in a Unique Setting

Would you choose to spend the night in jail? You might if it was this "olde jail." Through the bars of a heavy iron door, you enter into the sanctuary of the Taylors Falls Jail. An impressive pot belly stove, shiny and black, called Montana Queen warms the hearth even on the coldest day. You are diminished by the height of the ceiling. On the main walls a complete set of Burma shave signs are arranged with the jingle: Let Folks See How Bright You Are, Dim Your Lights Behind a Car-Burma Shave. You go for broke as you ascend the spiral staircase to the sleeping loft above. Is this for real? It's really fun! Al and Julie Kunz thought so when they bought the Old Jail House along with the adjacent Schottmuller Building from Helen White in 1989. Both structures are listed on the National Register of Historic Places. The jail is the oldest licensed bed and breakfast in the state of Minnesota.

The Schottmuller Building stood where the present-day Chisago House is located. It was moved to its new site on Government Road in 1868, because of a large cave located there that could store casks of beer at a cool sixty-eight degrees Fahrenheit for the Schottmuller Brewery. We twentieth-century citizens can enjoy the coolness of the space for different reasons. Cleverly located beneath the arch of the cave is a large claw-foot soaking tub for guests to enjoy by candlelight. A comfortable antique iron bed awaits your arrival, perhaps to read one of the many books provided for your fancy.

A suite of three rooms called the Playhouse is located on the upper floor of this building. Serendipitously arranged for your amusement are the many toys you might have remembered from your youth. Old crepe paper party hats decorate the walls. Childhood games such as Pin the Tail on the Donkey, Olle oop, Chinese checkers, and many more to tickle your fancy can be found. A glider swing is made into a sofa, and old-fashioned ice cream parlor cups sit at the table.

Red, white, and blue are the colors used to decorate throughout either in checks, solids, or country prints and florals.

All three suites have cozy kitchens well stocked with savory breakfast fixings ready to eat at your convenience. Microwaves are provided in each suite to warm things up. A basket of fresh breads, sweet rolls, and muffins are always given to guests. Potato pancakes and sausages are a specialty.

Centrally located in the heart of Taylors Falls, convenient to Interstate Park, river cruises, and other nearby recreational opportunities, The Old Jail Company proves to be an amusing venture.

~~~~~~~~~~~~~~~~

THE FACTS

THE OLD JAIL COMPANY

100 Government Rd., Taylors Falls, MN 55084. (612) 465-3112.

Innkeepers: Al and Julie Kunz. Established in 1989 as Old Jail Co., and in 1981 as Taylors Falls Jail House. Open year round.

Rooms: 3 separate suites. Baths: 3 pvt.

Cost: $90–$110 double. $30 less for second night with continental breakfast. Midweek and off-season discounts. Cash/personal checks.

Smoking permitted. No children. No pets.

Directions from Twin Cities: Take I-35 north to Hwy 8 exit east to downtown Taylors Falls. Left turn at bottom of hill entering Taylors Falls to Government Road.

*National Register of Historic Places

~~~~~~

THE BOATHOUSE BED AND BREAKFAST
A Cozy, Intimate Hideaway

Originally a boathouse for the older home situated on the adjacent lot, this white pine structure now serves as Minnesota's only "boathouse" bed and breakfast. You are on the shore of South Lindstrom Lake, and you can launch your own boat or enjoy the paddleboat provided by your hosts, Kathy and Randy Diers. Having moved to Lindstrom from Colorado in 1991, they purchased their lakeside home and the old boathouse. They felt this unique setting with lake access would be superb for a bed and breakfast.

In wintertime, you can cross-country ski or skate across the lake, then return to your own private retreat to stoke a fire while you sip a glass of wine, compliments of the Diers. Prepare your own picnic or dinner and enjoy it lakeside on the spacious deck. The comfortable quarters are neatly decorated, with all your needs served in this homey space—including a full kitchen, TV, and VCR.

Breakfast is served at your convenience in the boathouse dining area. Choice of beverages, fresh fruit of the season, cereal, and home-baked bread and muffins are the fare.

During the warmer months of the year, the boathouse is handicap accessible. The bathroom also features support bars for the handicapped.

~~~~~~~~~~~~~~~~

THE FACTS

THE BOATHOUSE BED AND BREAKFAST

30425 Vine St., Lindstrom, MN 55045. (612) 257-9122.

Innkeepers: Randy and Kathy Diers.

Rooms: 1 boathouse with fireplace & pvt. bath.

Cost: $89 weekends. $79 midweek (Sun-Thr). 10% less for stay of 2 or more consecutive nights. Cash/ personal or traveler's check. MC/Visa/Amex.

Smoke free. AC. Children welcome. No pets.

Directions from Twin Cities: Take I-35 north to exit 132 to Hwy 8. Go 11.5 miles to Lindstrom. Right turn on Vine St. Follow to lake. From Wisconsin: Take Hwy 8 west to Lindstrom.

~~~~~~

RED PINE BED & BREAKFAST
An Inspiration of Handcrafted Charm

When I was first told the Red Pine story, it struck me how remarkable these folks, Lowell and Gloria Olson, were. To dream a nearly impossible dream of handcrafting one's own log home and fulfilling that dream — as evidenced by this extraordinary home — is inspirational. Right from the selection of the logs, transporting them, arranging and stripping them of their bark, hand-fitting and reassembling them right down to the large ridgepole, painstakingly sanding and varnishing miles of decking, the entire Olson family persevered until completion.

And we are richer for it as they have opened their red pine log home in North Branch, Minnesota, to share with their bed and breakfast guests.

Of the many notable features of this home, I was most impressed by its breadth and height. The Great Room, with its majestic twenty-six-foot-high pine plank ceiling and split fieldstone chimney, is a blend of rough hewn with elegance. Queen Anne high-back upholstered chairs and a sofa with graceful curves have the look of country gentility. Each of these elements play off each other throughout the entire two-and-a-half story home.

The two spacious guest rooms are on the uppermost gallery level. Sharing a full-sized bathroom, the rooms are almost mirror images of each other. Both have sixteen-foot-high ceilings, French doors leading to your room, skylights, balconies overlooking the woods, and queensize brass beds. Table and chairs for private dining and turndown service is provided by Gloria, a very attentive innkeeper.

Breakfast can be arranged in your room or at the dining table in the Great Room. A more than satisfying meal was served to me and consisted of a fritatta of sausage and cheese with salsa on the side, fruit compote of pears served in yoghurt with a brown sugar and raisin sauce, a bran muffin, orange juice, and coffee.

Explore the private trails on these thirty wooded acres by foot in the summertime and cross-country skis in the winter.

Coming in the fall of '93 is a private guest room on the second level with its own entrance and private bath with whirlpool tub.

~~~~~~~~~~~~~~~~

THE FACTS
THE RED PINE BED AND BREAKFAST
15140 400th Street, North Branch, MN 55056. (612) 583-3326. Innkeepers: Lowell and Gloria Olson. Established in 1988. Open year round.
Rooms: 3 Baths: 1 shared - 1 pvt. with whirlpool tub.
Cost: $80–125 dbl. Inquire for business, senior and special Thur. rates.

Cash/personal or traveler's checks.

Smoke free. AC. No children or pets.

Directions from Twin Cities: Take I-35 north to N. Branch exit. Take Hwy 95 east 9 miles to County 70. Turn left or north. Travel l.5 miles to 400th St. and turn right. Red Pine is .25 miles on left.

~~~~~~

TREE TOP HEIGHTS BED & BREAKFAST
On the Millpond at Balsam Lake

Pat and Harvey Weberg found themselves with an empty nest when they moved to this three bedroom rambler seven years ago. They had heard people were sleeping in their cars when they couldn't find rooms at the local motels. They thought it would be great fun to have a bed and breakfast, so they applied for licensing and opened their home to guests in 1988. Pat tells me she has enjoyed it all, and they have had many guests from all over the world.

The Fourth of July Parade in Balsam Lake, craft show, and thrilling fireworks display over the lake is a fun time that brings many people to the area in the summer months. They find this an accommodating and pleasant home in which to stay while visiting. Two rooms on the lower level share a full-size bathroom and sitting area with desk and TV.

Breakfast is served in the dining room, which looks out at the deck. One seems to be on top of the trees as the rear yard slopes steeply to the millpond. The millpond at one time was a holding area for logs during the lumber boom. A full hearty breakfast is served including pancakes, waffles, or french toast with fresh fruit, rolls, juice, and coffee.

For additional pleasure, guests are favored with the use of a boat, canoe, pair of bikes, and hammock for idling away an afternoon. Since this home is just a short distance away from the Polk County Museum, the bikes might be a handy way to travel there.

~~~~~~~~~~~~~~~~~~

THE FACTS

TREE TOP HEIGHTS BED AND BREAKFAST

Rt. 1, Box 634, Indianhead Shores, Balsam Lake, WI 54810.

(715) 485-3433.

Innkeepers: Pat and Harvey Weberg. Established l988. Open year round.

Rooms: 2   Bath: 1 shared

Cost: $45 double. Cash/personal checks.

No smoking. AC. Accommodate children over 10 years.

Directions: In WI take Hwy 8 east to Hwy 46 north; take Hwy 46 to Balsam Lake. Turn right onto 4th Ave. and take to Indianhead Shores Dr.; turn left and go .1 mile.

~~~~~~

GANDY DANCER BED AND BREAKFAST
Named for Old Railroad Workers

Jim and Vivian Snyder chose a wonderful rolling meadow with a perimeter of red oak and maple as the setting for their modern, two-story dwelling eight years ago. It is located just three hundred yards from the Gandy Dancer Trail, a recreational trail running along an abandoned railroad line, from which this B&B also takes its name. A gandy dancer was a railroad worker, so called because as a worker laid the track it appeared that he was dancing, and the tools he used were made by the Gandy Co.

The couple love to tell the story of how they worked together to build their passive solar home. Their setting is unique on these ten wooded acres. One is easily distracted by the welcoming views outside the expansive south-facing window walls or the east side deck and sun porch.

On the lower level you'll find a great room divided by a large open stairway. One end serves as library and TV viewing area, while a woodstove with glass doors and comfortable his-and-her chairs provide a warm and restful location. The lower level guest room is adjacent to this area and contains a double bed. On the upper level a larger bedroom with queensize bed and family heirlooms is located near the three season porch. Guests share one and a half bathrooms.

Breakfast is served on the dining room table overlooking woods and the lower level. Sausage and french toast topped with Vivian's own hot cinnamon syrup is a favorite among guests. Also served are fresh fruit and choice of beverages, of course.

As recreational opportunities increase on the trail (presently, the trail is used for snowmobiling in winter) that is, the trail is resurfaced for the silent sports (biking and rollerblading), this B & B offers an ideal rest at trail's end.

~~~~~~~~~~~~~~~~
THE FACTS
GANDY DANCER BED AND BREAKFAST
P.O. Box 563, Frederic, WI 54837. (715) 327-8750.
Innkeepers: Jim and Vivian Snyder. Established 1992. Open year round.
Rooms: 2 Baths: 1-1/2
Cost: $40 double. Cash/personal or traveler's checks.
Smoke free. AC. Inquire about children. No pets.
Directions: 1 mile north of Frederic, WI, on Hwy 35. Left onto 150th St. for .7 mile; cross bridge and turn right.

~~~~~~

SEVEN PINES LODGE*
Trout Dinners and Fly Fishing at Historic Lodge

A man with a commitment to the natural surroundings of the white pine timberlands and a passion for fly fishing bought nearly 680 acres in upper Polk County in the state of Wisconsin. This man, a multimillionaire, sportsman, and former mayor of Hudson, Wisconsin, was Charles Lewis. After making his fortune in grain from humble beginnings, he grabbed his chance at preserving a piece of history. His lodge at Lewis, Wisconsin, was completed in 1903, handcrafted with simple tools and made of pine logs.

A natural spring-fed trout stream is stocked with 5,500 rainbow and brook trout per mile. This is a catch-and-release stream and is open for fishing all year long.

The lodge consists of several buildings: the main lodge, Carriage House, Stream House, and Gate House. The main lodge has five guest rooms, one private bath, and two shared; the Carriage House has two bedrooms and shared bath. The Stream House is a perfectly square building with a unique wraparound veranda buttressed by large brackets; it is built next to the stream but creates an illusion of being over the stream. It has a private bath. The Gate House, formerly Lewis's office, has a fireplace, Adirondack bed, and whirlpool. It is popular among honeymoon couples.

The main lodge is filled with precious antiques and treasures of the past and has a wealthy sportsman's air of decoration. Long comfortable sofas and slightly worn oriental carpets blend well with the more rustic elements of the lodge. President Calvin C. Coolidge slept in the lodge; that event is memorialized in the President's Room.

The story of Seven Pines is not complete without the source of its name. Apparently when the lodge was constructed seven large white pines of great maturity (nearly two hundred years old at the time) towered over it. Three remain today, the elements of nature have taken their toll on the rest. Seven Pines is now on the National Register of Historic Places.

A continental breakfast is served in the dining room in the main lodge.

Besides serving as a bed and breakfast on the weekends, this lodge accommodates business meetings and retreats as well as special parties.

~~~~~~~~~~~~~
THE FACTS

THE SEVEN PINES LODGE
P.O. Box 137, Lewis, WI 54851. (715) 653-2323.
Proprietor: Lee Gohlike. Mgr: Mary Bayliss. Open year round on weekends as a bed and breakfast. Established 1932 as a lodge.

Rooms: 5 in main lodge; 2-bedroom suite in Carriage House; 1 in Stream House; 1-bedroom suite in Gate House. Baths: 2 shared in main lodge; 1 shared in Carriage House; private baths in Stream and Gate Houses.
Cost: $74–$150 double. MC/Visa/cash/personal checks.
Smoking in designated areas only. AC. Children welcome. No pets.
Directions: Take Hwy 35 in WI north of Frederic to Lewis.

*National Register of Historic Places

~~~~~~

FORGOTTEN TYMES COUNTRY INN
White Pine Logs and Country All the Way

When Al and Pat Blume decide upon doing something they do it all the way. They have lived on their 153-acre farm in Siren, Wisconsin, for sixteen years and have been doing something to it every year. They started with the main lodge, which they constructed of white pine logs on the site of the old farm house. Throughout you find antiques and comfortable furnishings. An immense brick hearth, accommodated by a high vaulted ceiling, dominates the kitchen. A vintage cast-iron-and-enamel Universal gas cookstove is sometimes used for canning. You can sit on the deck outside the kitchen and overlook pool, lake, and gardens. A guest room with private bathroom sleeps four in this main house.

All guests take their continental style breakfast in the main house dining area. A full breakfast is available for an extra charge.

The Blumes decided on a blend of the past with conveniences of the present to set the theme for their country style inn. To them the past represented unhurried times for observing nature's simple treats.

They went about finding a 125-year-old log cabin, purchased it, marked the logs, dismantled it, and brought the logs to this site. Then they set about reconstructing what they now call the Trapper's Cabin. With a wraparound deck, wide plank pine floors, country antiques, woodburning stove, and many artifacts of the "old fur trappers" of the region, the cabin speaks of forgotten times. Three king-size beds sleep six comfortably. The cabin has a large, full bath with shower.

But success with that venture spurred them on to expand, and soon they added the Stable, which was built above an old log barn. At the Stable, try your hand at pool, sleep in a barn stall, and eat on a long wooden handyman's grub table. This is a unique space for a gathering, as this building sleeps up to ten. There are three bathrooms and one Jacuzzi room here.

The Blumes next moved what was the first church school of Webster, Wisconsin, onto their farm and reconstructed the Old Schoolhouse for their guests. This is a barrier-free, handicap-accessible cabin that sleeps up to eight and has two bathrooms.

Yet another project is in the works as Al and Pat are constructing the

Honeymoon Cabin. Designed as a romantic and comfortable lodging with a king-size bed and double Jacuzzi, this promises to be an attractive getaway for two.

Apart from their mastery at recycling old log structures, the Blumes have a capacity for exceptional carpentry as they have handcrafted all of the beds at Forgotten Tymes from rough-sawn pine two-by-fours. Their signature on each bed is a cut out white pine at the headboard. Down comforters and pillows, flannel sheets in winter, and embroidered eyelet in summer dress all of the beds. Other amenities common to all are the community sauna, TV, VCR, and telephones in each cabin.

Since the whole farm is situated on Long Lake, fishing, boating, and swimming are easily accessible. Bring your own boat or use the kayaks and canoes at the farm. The farm boasts two Norwegian Fjord horses—mother and baby. A male Clydesdale, Bud, provides sleigh rides in winter.

~~~~~~~~~~~~~~~~

THE FACTS

FORGOTTEN TYMES COUNTRY INN BED AND BREAKFAST
Tower Rd., Siren, WI 54872. (715) 349-5837.
Innkeepers: Al and Pat Blume. Established 1991. Open year round.
Rooms: 1 in main house. Bath: Pvt.
Trappers Cabin: Sleeping loft sleeps six. Bath: 1 shared.
Schoolhouse: 3 sets of twins. Bath: 2 shared.
Stable: 4 bedrooms sleep 10. Bath: 3 shared. One Jacuzzi room.
Honeymoon: 1 bedroom. Bath: Pvt. with double whirlpool.
Cost: $79.95–$95 double. Each additional is $30. Special rates upon inquiry. All major credit cards.
Limited smoking. Handicap accessible. AC. Children and pets welcome. Additional fee for pets.
Directions: Located on Tower Rd. in Siren, WI, directly off of Hwy 35. About 90 miles from the Twin Cities and 60 miles from Duluth/Superior.

~~~~~~

AUNT MARTHA'S GUEST HOUSE
Where Lasting Friendships Are Made

Lasting friendships are made at this Spooner, Wisconsin, country bed and breakfast owing to the affable and gracious nature of its hostess Mary Askov. Taking pleasure in meeting and having guests, Mary is obviously a hostess one does not forget.

In 1990 she was happy to start her B & B, selecting the name "Aunt Martha" in loving memory of her sister. Formerly this was a country post office and originally a general store erected in 1927 by a Glen Marsh.

Simplicity and rustic charm prevail in this old-fashioned decorated home. Handmade patchwork quilts, handloomed floor mats, filmy sheer window curtains, and memorabilia create a special kind of homey

charm. All three guest rooms have that down home comfort. Children travel-
ing with parents can be accommodated in the second floor guest room, which
contains a trundle bed. The main floor guest room has a full-sized brass bed
and attached private bath. The upstairs guest rooms share a bathroom.

Breakfast is served at the convenience of guests in front of the window
looking out at the front porch. Pancakes or french toast accompanied by
honey produced from a nearby hive tended by the ancestors of this home
might be your fare. Fresh fruit and juices along with coffee and tea are also
served.

Five miles northwest is Voyager Village Country Club, a seven-thousand-
acre recreational area for golfing, swimming, and tennis.

~~~~~~~~~~~~~~~~

THE FACTS

AUNT MARTHA'S GUEST HOUSE
1602 County Rd. A, Spooner, WI 54801. (715) 635-6857.
Innkeeper: Mary Askov. Established 1990. Open year round.
Rooms: 3 Baths: 1 shared and 1 pvt.
Cost: $45–$55 double. Cash/personal or traveler's checks. Smoke free. Children welcome.
No pets.
Directions: Take WI Hwy 35 to Siren. Hwy 70 east to County H. Left on H several miles
to Old Road A, then right on Old Road A.

~~~~~~

WILDFLOWER - A BED & BREAKFAST
Doll Collectors Will Love It

The love of dolls is a language universal to the young and young-at-heart.
In this contemporary rustic style home, I was surprised to find an exquisite
collection of dolls that innkeeper Nancy Likes has been gathering for twenty
years. Once in her keep, Nancy doesn't allow the dolls to gather dust but
enjoys displaying them in whimsical positions here and there as if they might
be a guest at her house. From lavish lace, satins, and bows, her dolls are also
dressed by costumes stitched by Nancy. All of these treasured heirlooms elegantly combined with the charming rustic setting create a rich sense of senti-
ment and style.

On the main level chairs are carefully arranged to invite conversation near
the fieldstone hearth. On the level below, a distinctive fireplace has been created from St. Croix riverbed rock, and found objects have been imbedded in
the mortar as another reminder of sentiments of the past. A pair of attractive
guest rooms on the lower level share a large bathroom. As you pass up the
stairs off the main room, you are on your way to another pair of guest rooms
that share another larger bathroom. Romantic and attractive furnishings com-
bine, creating a pleasant place to end your day.

A former pastry chef at the White Bear Yacht Club and presently chef at a
nearby facility for girls, Nancy takes pride in preparing "everything from
scratch." Her breakfasts, served in the dining room, are hearty and scrump-
tious. She prepared a vegetable-and-meat filled omelette for me, served with
fresh fruits including cantaloupe and strawberries, toasted sunflower seed

bread, orange juice, and coffee.

Wildflower is located just one mile from Forts Folle Avoine (an historical fur trading post) near hiking, horseback, and many other recreational trails.

~~~~~~~~~~~~~~~~

THE FACTS

WILDFLOWER - A BED AND BREAKFAST
8375 N. Bass Lake Rd., Danbury, WI 54830. (715) 656-4210.
Innkeeper: Nancy Likes. Established 1993. Open year round.
Rooms: 4   Baths: 2 shared.
Cost: $45–$65 double. Cash/personal or traveler's checks. Limited smoking. AC. Children welcome. No pets.
Directions: Take Hwy 35 in WI to 5 miles south of Danbury. Turn west onto County Rd. U. Take to East Bass Lake Rd., where you turn right. Wildflower is on the left about 2 miles down the road.

~~~~~~

DAKOTA LODGE
Elegant Haven of Privacy

Don't be fooled by the rustic exterior of the Dakota Lodge in Hinckley, Minnesota. Soon after you enter this half pine log-sided edifice, your eyes tell you differently. Stepping into a spacious salon elegantly furnished with oriental carpets and hardwood floors, a pair of quality sofas, carefully chosen antiques, and tiled fireplace, your disposition becomes relaxed.

Former North Dakotans, Tad Hilborn and Michael Smitz purchased what was a former "nite club" built to showcase the talents of "Krissy," who billed herself as the "last of the red hot mamas." In 1991 the building underwent major restoration work, mostly accomplished by Mike and Tad, and what emerged was the Dakota Lodge. They saw this as becoming a "place for privacy and comfort." Continuing the process of transformation, they have recently created only five guest suites, four of which have fireplaces and double whirlpool baths and private toilets. The one remaining room, Eastedge (a value at fifty-five dollars per night), has a private tub, shower, and toilet, but you need to walk down the hall a bit to get there. Each suite is tastefully decorated and of sufficient size with queensize beds.

Breakfast is served in the classically decorated eighteenth-century style dining room. Typically you might have scrambled eggs with cream and chives, french toast, bacon, sausage, fresh fruit, and choice of beverages. Complimentary beverages are served from two to eight in the evening daily.

A ten percent discount is given for stays of more than three nights. While not a barrier-free environment, everything here is on one level, so easy access to rooms and other services is accomplished.

~~~~~~~~~~~~~~~~

THE FACTS

THE DAKOTA LODGE - A BED AND BREAKFAST
Rt. 3, Box 178, Hinckley, MN 55037. (612) 384-6052.
Innkeepers: Tad Hilborn and Mike Smitz. Established 1991. Open year round.
Rooms: 5; 4 with fireplaces. Baths: 5 pvt.; 4 with whirlpools.

Cost: $55–$110 double. MC/Visa/Discover/cash/personal or traveler's checks. Limited smoking. AC. No children or pets. Easy access for wheelchair bound.
Directions from Twin Cities: Take I-35 north to Hinckley. Take Hwy 48 east 10 miles to lodge.

~~~~~~

THE VICTORIAN ROSE BED & BREAKFAST*
Turn-of-the-Century Style in the Country

Hardly a resident of Finlayson, Minnesota, wouldn't know the story of John Oldenberg. This Finnish immigrant, conversant in seven languages, found his talents put to use when the railroads expanded into the northwest; he was employed to purchase land for their expansion. In 1896 he built a classic revival home for his bride on this three-acre site overlooking pond and lake and called it the "Villa Blanca." Now painted shades of tan, cream, and burnt orange, the present owners Tom and Su Ann O'Brien have restored this home to the style of its heyday, when Mr. Oldenberg entertained frequently. Tom O'Brien related that "Oldenberg was quite the political animal."

Upon entering the reception area you notice the portieres that hang at the entrance of the main parlor and dining room. Antique furnishings, oriental carpets, and Victorian-era wallpapers decorate the first floor. The ambience is romantic. Up on the second floor there are three guest rooms. The O'Briens have provided comfortable, impressive antique beds for their guests.

A high-back oak sleigh bed with matching dresser and dressing table grace the Green Room. You'll have a view of the lake in the Blue Room, which is accented with white wicker rocker and table and a high-back oak bed dressed in crisp white linens. These rooms share a bath with whirlpool. The Rose Room, a two-room suite containing a walnut Renaissance revival bed and other antiques, has a private bath with shower. The pedestal sink has unique soda fountain handles manufactured at around 1910 by the Chicago Brass Co.— such fun to use! Su Ann loves collecting old period costumes and carefully displays these ensembles either on forms or as wall hangings.

Breakfast is served either in the dining room or on the front porch. Eggs Benedict or baked frittata are some of Su Ann's favorite fixings for a hearty breakfast, served along with fresh fruit or apple crisp, breads and coffee cake, and choice of beverage.

Upon arrival guests might be treated to some choice dessert such as apple pie. Su Ann likes to place fresh-cut roses in the rooms as their signature.

Guests will find this a pleasant location as the gardens are inviting. Take a walk around the pond or skate on it when frozen. This bed and breakfast is also convenient to the Hinckley Fire State Trail for cyclists.

~~~~~~~~~~~~~~~~

THE FACTS
THE VICTORIAN ROSE BED & BREAKFAST
2230 Hwy 18, Finlayson, MN 55375. (612) 233-7531 or 572-8041.
Innkeepers: Tom & Su Ann O'Brien. Established in 1991. Open year round, weekends.
Rooms: 3   Baths: 1 pvt., 1 shared with whirlpool.
Cost: $50 shared bath; $70 pvt. bath. Cash/personal or traveller's checks.

Smoke free. AC. Inquire about children. No pets.
Directions: Take I-35 north in Minnesota to exit 195. Go west to County 18, then four miles to Finlayson.

* National Register of Historic Places
~~~~~~

THE STOUT TROUT BED & BREAKFAST
Wildlife and Sunsets on Gull Lake

Kathy Fredericks moved back to Wisconsin in 1986 with a bed and breakfast in mind. Having grown up some sixty miles south of her present home on Gull Lake, Kathy purchased what was the old Stilson resort (a forty-acre site) and refurbished the main lodge building, which dates back to the late nineteenth century.

Her experiences as a well-travelled person are reflected in the many interesting decorative accessories in the home. Wonderful North African baskets decorate the stairway to the second floor. All the wide plank floors are painted to match the theme of the guest rooms, which are a comfortable size and cheerfully decorated, each containing some whimsical wooden sculpture by local artist Don Gahr. Use the rear balcony for stargazing or watching the deer come down the meadow at dusk as you wait for the sunset.

Breakfast is served at your convenience in front of a large window in the dining room, on a table top that has been wonderfully painted by Kathy to reflect the natural surroundings and wildlife you might discover at the Stout Trout. Homemade maple syrup on pancakes with sausages, fresh fruit, and wild berries make up a hearty breakfast served here.

Guests can come here with modest or great expectations. Have great expectations if you plan to be involved in the activities of the environment, which is rich with the possibilities of fishing, horseback riding, cross-country skiing, or boating. Or you may choose to do little more than curl up to read a book on the deck overlooking the lake, or just meander through the woods. Kathy has provided a place to store your fishing and skiing gear, and there are boats and cycles for guests to use.

~~~~~~~~~~~~~~~~
THE FACTS
THE STOUT TROUT BED & BREAKFAST
Rt. 1, Box 1630, Springbrook, WI 54875-9611. (715) 466-2790.
Innkeeper: Kathy Fredricks. Established 1987. Open year round.
Rooms: 4   Baths: 4 pvt.
Cost: $65 double. Cash/personal or traveler's checks.
Smoke free. Fans; no AC. No children; no pets.
Directions: Take WI Hwy 53 about 6 miles north of Trego to County Rd. F. Take F 3.5 miles east to Stout Trout.
~~~~~~

NOTES

NOTES

*The charming dining room
at Amberwood Bed and Breakfast in St. Croix Falls.*

*Janet's Room is named for the innkeeper's sister who stitched the
quilt and curtains for the room.*

A charming pair , innkeepers, Lois and Bud Barott of the Country Bed and Breakfast of Shafer, MN.

The Lavender Room.

The Country Estate Room.

Vàr (Spring) a lovely ivy-stenciled guest room.

Höst (Autumn), this guest room has a handcrocheted bedcover.

Some of the country charm you'll find at the Old Franconia Hotel Bed and Breakfast, Shafer, MN.

The Cottage Bed and Breakfast in Taylors Falls has a premier view of the river and the valley.

The main level of the guest suite at The Cottage.

Cindy's Study — a guest room at the McLane House Bed and Breakfast in Taylors Falls.

The Jail (a guest suite) at the Old Jail Co. Bed and Breakfast in Taylors Falls. Note the Montana Queen pot-bellied stove.

The Boathouse, a Bed and Breakfast on the shores of South
Lindstrom Lake in Lindstrom, MN

A very comfortable retreat with a fireplace and views of the lake.

The Red Pine Bed and Breakfast, a family built log home in North Branch.

The Great Room with its high vaulted ceiling.

Spacious guest room with brass bed, dining and sitting areas.

Tree Top Heights Bed and Breakfast, located on the Millpond in Balsam Lake, WI.

Gandy Dancer Bed and Breakfast, Frederic, WI. A passive solar home with south facing window walls.

*Stream House at
Seven Pines Lodge
in Lewis, WI.*

*Dining area on the back porch
of the Main Lodge.*

*The President's Room at the
Main Lodge.*

*Detail from hand painted glass win-
dow of front door at Main Lodge.*

*Trapper's Cabin
at Forgotten Tymes
Bed and Breakfast
in Siren, WI.*

Elegant country furnishings and antiques in the cabin.

*Handcrafted
beds in all
sleeping areas.*

The table is set for breakfast.

Aunt Martha's Guest House in Spooner, WI.

St. Croix River rock used in this fireplace at Wildflower Bed and Breakfast in Danbury, WI.

Part of a collection, this fine German doll sits prettily as breakfast is served at Wildflower.

The Dakota Lodge in Hinckley, MN. Note the elegance of the living room pictured below.

The Medora Room, named for a resurrected tourist area of North Dakota, has all the comforts.

The main parlor of the Victorian Rose
Bed and Breakfast in Finlayson, MN.

Pictured is the Blue Room of the above
B & B, with its crisp white linens.

The Stout Trout Bed and Breakfast
in Springbrook, WI sits on the
shores of the peaceful Gull Lake,
below.

List of Chambers of Commerce and Other Business Associations

Afton Village Business Assn.
P.O. Box 102
Afton, MN 55001

Baldwin Area Chamber of
Commerce
P.O. Box 142
Baldwin, WI 54002

Balsam Lake Community Club
P.O. Box 366
Balsam Lake, WI 54810

Burnett County Dept. of
Tourism and Information
P.O. Box 560, Hwy 35 N
Siren, WI 54872

Chisago Lakes Area Chamber of
Commerce
P.O. Box 283
Lindstrom, MN 55045

Frederic Area Community Assn.
106 S. Wisconsin Ave.
Frederic, WI 54837

Hastings Area Chamber of
Commerce
1304 Vermillion St.
Hastings, MN 55033

Hinckley Area Chamber of
Commerce
P.O. Box 189
Hinckley, MN 55037

Hudson Area Chamber of
Commerce
429 Second St.
Hudson, WI 54016

Osceola Business Assn.
201 2nd Ave.
Osceola, WI 54020

Pine County Tourist Assn.
705 Hillside Avenue
Pine City, MN 55063

Polk County Business & Tourism
Assn.
Polk County Courthouse
Balsam Lake, WI 54810

Prescott Area Chamber of
Commerce
121 Broad St.
Prescott, WI 54021

River Falls Area Chamber
of Commerce
115 East Elm Street
River Falls, WI 54022

St. Croix Falls Area Chamber of
Commerce
P.O. Box 178
St. Croix Falls, WI 54024

Stillwater Area Chamber
of Commerce
423 S. Main St.
Stillwater, MN 55082

Taylors Falls Chamber of
Commerce
333 Bench St.
Taylors Falls, MN 55084

Washburn County Dept.
of Tourism - Jim Hagen
Sarona, WI 54870

Minnesota Office of Tourism
275 Jackson St.
St. Paul, MN 55101-1848

Wisconsin Division of Tourism
123 W. Washington Ave.
Madison, WI 53703

St. Croix Valley Area Information Guide to Fine Dining, Special Attractions and Specialty Stores

FINE DINING

The Bayport American Cookery
328 5th Avenue North, Bayport, Mn. 55003.
(612) 430-1066.
Lunch, Mon.- Fri. Dinner: Wed., Thur., & Sun. one seating at 6:30 p.m. Dinner: Fri. & Sat. (3 seatings) 6:00 p.m., 7:30 p.m., & 8:30 p.m. A casual, intimate dining room combined with exquisite food has made this restaurant a priority selection in special occasion dining. Featured is a five course fixed price menu for dinner and an a la carte menu for lunch. Full beverage service.

The Brunswick Inn
114 E. Chestnut St., Stillwater, Mn. 55082
(612) 430-2653 or (800) 828-2653
Dinner: Friday and Saturday nights at 7:15 p.m. (one seating). Romance and opulence are the rules of the evening in this Mid-Victorian dining room located in Stillwater's oldest structure. Featured is a fixed price High-Victorian multi-course dinner. Fine domestic wines and specialty beers.

Dalles House Restaurant
Hwy 8 and 35, St. Croix Falls, WI 54024
(800) 643-7412 or (715) 483-3246
7 a.m. to 10 p.m. Casual fine dining. Breakfast, lunch and dinner. Daily specials, fresh seafood. Noted for their fresh baked "huge" popovers.

Esteban's Restaurant and Cantina
324 S. Main St., Stillwater, Mn. 55082
(612) 430-1543.
Open daily 11:00 a.m. to 1:00 a.m. Savor the sights, scents and sensational sauces of Mexican and Southwest American cuisine. Lunch buffet daily, also Wednesday evening dinner buffet and Sunday brunch buffet.

The Gasthaus Bavarian Hunter
8390 Lofton Ave., Stillwater, MN 55082
(612) 439-7128. Located in a beautiful rural Stillwater setting, this authentic German restaurant has been serving Bavarian specialties since 1966. Imported beers, wines and liquors. Open daily for lunch and dinner year round.

The Historic Afton House Inn
3291 S. St. Croix Trail, P.O. Box 326, Afton, MN
(612) 436-8883. Sunday: brunch 10 a.m. to 2 p.m., dinner: 4:00 p.m.-9:00 p.m., Mon.- Sat. 5:00 p.m. to 11:00 p.m. Full service fine dining. Specializing in flaming tableside entrées and desserts.

Jacques Place
188 Front St., Prescott, WI 54021. (715) 262-4200
Open daily for lunch and dinner. Northern Italian cuisine with creative and interesting specialties. Featuring seafood, fresh soups, breads and imported cheeses. A fine selection of domestic wines. Located on the riverfront.

Organica Restaurant at the Aveda Spa Retreat
1015 Cascade St., Osceola, WI 54020. (800) AVEDA02 or (715) 294-4465
Please call the spa for hours and reservations. (One hour drive from Minneapolis). Organica Restaurant at the Aveda Spa Retreat features an appealing menu of impeccably fresh and flavorful organic foods served in the spa's sun porch or private dining room overlooking acres of natural beauty.

Savories
108 North Main St., Stillwater, MN 55082
(612) 430-0702. Tues-Thur. 7 a.m.-6 p.m.; Fri. 7 a.m.-9 p.m.; Sat. 8 a.m.-9 p.m. and Sun. 8 a.m.-6 p.m. Stillwater's own unique and original casual dining. Featuring homemade soups and other delectables. Creative dinners served a la carte change weekly. Wine and micro-beers. Full service catering available.

Steamboat Inn
307 Lake St. North, Prescott, WI 54021
(800) 262-8232 or (715) 262-5858. Lunch, Mon-Fri. (May-Oct.). Dinner, Mon.-Sat. Chicken and fish fry on Fri. eve. Sunday breakfast and lunch buffet 10-2 p.m. Sunday dinner starting at noon. Fine dining overlooking the beautiful St. Croix River. Enjoy appetizers and cocktails on the veranda. Extensive menu. Closed Mondays Oct.-April.

Vittorio's (Grotto Blue)
402 S. Main St. (P.O. Box 437) Stillwater, MN 55082.
(612) 439-3588. Open from 5:00 p.m. to 10:00 p.m. (Sun-Thu), 5:00 p.m. to mid-nite (Fr-Sa). Specializing in homemade pasta and northern Italian cuisine. "Original cave surroundings create a most elegant dining atmosphere."

SPECIAL ATTRACTIONS

Afton Cruise Lines
3291 S. St. Croix Trail, Afton, MN 55001
P.O. Box 326. (612) 436-8883. Public Sunday Champagne
Brunch Cruise. Noon to 2 p.m. May to October.

Aveda Spa Retreat
1015 Cascade St., Osceola, WI 54020
800-AVEDA02 (283-3202) or (715) 294-4465
Aveda Spa Retreat in Osceola, Wisconsin has extensive spa, body, beauty treatments, gourmet organic food and beautiful surroundings. Packages, seminars and group retreats available. Open year round. Please call for reservations and directions.

Bass Lake Cheese Factory
598 Valley View Trail, Somerset, WI
(800) 368-2437. Mon.-Fri. 10-6 , Sat. 10-5, and Sun. 11-5. Family owned and operated cheese factory with retail on premises. Cheeses made include goat and sheep milk cheeses. Colby and Jack cheeses from cow's milk.

The Drive-In
632 Bench St., Taylors Falls, MN 55084.
(612) 465-7831. Open Mid-April to mid-Oct., 10:30 a.m. to 10:30 p.m. Unique to the Valley, this 1950's built drive-in restaurant has car hops dressed in poodle skirts serving handpacked burgers and frosted mugs of root beer. Picnic area available.

Northern Vineyards Winery
402 North Main St., Stillwater, MN 55082
(612) 430-2012. Mon.- Sat. 10 a.m.-5 p.m. Sun. Noon - 5 p.m. A functioning winery, located in the historic Isaac Staples Mill. Featuring table wines made from Minnesota grown grapes. Free wine tasting daily.

St. Croix Casino and Hotel
Turtle Lake, Wisconsin
(800) 846-8946 or (800) U-GO-U-WIN. Open 24 hours daily. Northern Wisconsin's premier casino with an adjacent 159 room hotel. 700 loose slot machines and 32 Blackjack tables.

St. Croix Custom Cruises
8333 Mitchell Rd., Eden Prairie, Mn. 55334
(612) 949-9634. Cruise the scenic St. Croix River from May 15 to Oct. 15. Friday night Pizza Party, 7 p.m. departure, includes pizza, beer and pop. $15.00 plus tax per person. Sunday Brunch, 11 a.m. departure, includes 2-hour cruise and superb brunch buffet. $17.95 plus tax per person. Cruises depart from Afton, Minnesota.

Vittorio's Wolf Brewery Caves
402 S. Main St. (P.O. Box 437)
Stillwater, Mn. 55082. (612) 439-3588. Open Tues. to Sun. from Memorial Day to Labor Day. 9,000 square feet of hand dug caves which were part of the former Jos. Wolf Brewery. Guided tours. Groups welcome. Fee.

SPECIALTY STORES

Abigail Page Antique Emporium
503 Second St., Hudson, WI 54016. (715) 386-1505. Open Mon-Sat from 10 a.m. to 6 p.m., Friday until 7 p.m. Sundays noon - 5 p.m. Multi-dealer antique mall located in "old Town" Hudson.

Gustaf's and Gustaf's World of Christmas
13045 Lake Blvd. Box 722. Lindstrom, MN 55045.
(800) 831-8413. Open from 9:30 a.m. to 5:30 p.m. on Mon. through Sat. Fri. evenings til 8:30 p.m. Sunday noon to 5 p.m. Gift and collectible shop and year round Christmas store. Wonderful items and decorations. Located in historic building on National Register.

The Iris Art Gallery
Hwy 8 and Co. Rd. 25., Lindstrom, MN 55045
(800) 877-9509. Mon.-Fri. 11 a.m.-6 p.m. Sat. & Sun. 11 a.m. to 5 p.m. Located in an historic 1885 home, this gallery features the original art of Minnesota artists in oils, watercolors, pastels, sculpture, pottery etc. Exhibitions are ongoing with 'special exhibitions' changing about every six weeks. Schedule of exhibitions available.

Mulberry Point Antiques
270 N. Main St., Stillwater, MN 55082
(612) 430-3630. Open daily all year. 10 a.m. to 6 p.m. 65 quality antique dealers on four bright and spacious floors. One of six emporiums and several other dealers on historic Main Street of Stillwater.

Stone Cottage
1281 45th Ave., Amery, WI 54001
(715) 268-9515. Open all year. Wed.- Sat. 10 a.m.- 5 p.m. and Sunday from noon to 5 p.m. A unique fieldstone building nestled among tall pines, filled with country furniture, antiques and handicrafts. Many one of a kind items. From Amery, take County Hwy F west to Hwy C, then south on C for 3.5 miles.

SPECIAL EVENTS
(This is just a sampling of some of the events occurring in the St. Croix Valley. For specific dates please contact local area chambers of commerce)

JANUARY
Balloon Fest • **Lindstrom, MN** — Three-day event includes hot air balloon events and other celebrations.

Mid-winter National Snow Cross Snowmobile Race • **Siren, WI** — Two-day national competition.

FEBRUARY
Hot Air Affair • Hudson, WI — Three-day event includes hot air balloon events, fireworks and a parade.

Siren's Annual Waterskip • **Siren, WI** — Two-day event of national snowmobile water-cross competition. Held on Clam Lake.

MAY
Taste for Tulips • **Baldwin, WI** — Entertainment, Norwegian and Dutch foods. Held during traditional tulip times.

Rivertown Art Festival • **Stillwater, MN** — Weekend event includes arts and crafts of local artists.

JUNE
Frederic Family Days • **Frederic, WI** — Three-day event with entertainment, parade, fireworks and more.
Wannigan Days • **St. Croix Falls, WI** — Street dances with parade and car show.

Summerfolk Music Festival • **Hastings, MN** — Held at the Carpenter Nature Center.

Art in the Park • **Afton, MN** — Two-day event.

JULY
Booster Days • **Hudson, WI** — 4th of July celebration with carnival, bands, dances, parade, fireworks and more.

Freedom Festival • **Balsam, Lake, WI** — 4th of July celebration with boat parade, races, fireworks and more.

River Falls Days • **River Falls, WI** — Two-day event with a parade and other celebrations.

Rivertown Days Festival • **Hastings, MN** — Two-day event with parade, music festival, arts and crafts fair, fireworks and more.

Polk County Fair • **St. Croix Falls, WI** — Four-day event

Korn & Klover Karnival • **Hinckley, MN** — World champion marching bands are invited to perform. Parades, entertainment and midway.

Karl Oskar Days • **Lindstrom, MN** — Two-day event celebration of Swedish heritage.

AUGUST
Washington County Fair • **Stillwater, MN** — Four-day event.

St. Croix Valley Arts Council Art & Craft Fair • **St. Croix Falls, WI**

PepperFest • **North Hudson, WI** — Italian food, carnival, games and a parade.

Let's Go Dutch Days • **Baldwin, WI** — Three-day event, including Dutch foods, costumes and entertainment by the Klompen Dansers and the Kinder Klompers. Parade, flower and art show and much more.

Sheepdog Trials • **Taylors Falls, MN** — Sheepdog herding competitors gather here from throughout the U.S. for this annual event. A unique event.

Spelmansstamma • **Scandia, MN** — A true Swedish fiddling festival. It includes master fiddlers from all over, exhibitions, workshops and smorgasbord.

SEPTEMBER
Wings & Wheels • **Osceola, WI** — Antique car show, aircraft exhibit and Fly-In. Arts and crafts and more.

Valley Antique Show & Sale • **Stillwater, MN** — Two-day event held in the Stillwater Armory.

Rivertown Restoration Historic Home Tour • **Stillwater, MN** — One-day event.

OCTOBER
Leaf Spectacular • **Taylors Falls, MN** — Celebration of autumn colors from the last weekend in September through the first full weekend in October.

Rivertown Fall Colors Festival • **Stillwater, MN** — Held the first full fall weekend. A juried arts and crafts show of over 150 exhibitors.

NOVEMBER & DECEMBER
Victorian Christmas celebrations and lighting festivals are held throughout the Valley during the holiday season. Write or call the local area chambers of commerce to obtain information on specific events, dates and times.

In the Vale of the St. Croix*

I have sung of the glories of Switzerland.
I have talked of the treasures of Rome,
Of the wonderful marvelous glaciers,
And the beauty of Cant'y Scotch Home.
But I'm glad of a surcease of labor,
From besetments that vex and annoy;
And I drink in the glory of Nature
Along the shores of our lovely St. Croix.

I enjoyed each foot of the Trossacks,
The mountains of Wales were sublime,
While the beautiful gardens of Berlin
Are a blessing for all coming time.
I am glad the journey is over,
And I laugh like a rollicking boy,
As I feast on the splendor of beauty
Along the vale of the lovely St. Croix.

I've studied the glory of color,
From the picture of Raphael divine;
I've recited the time honored legends
As we drift by the shores of the Rhine.
But I hope when I've ended my journey,
God will grant me this fullness of joy–
Just to rest in my beatiful garden
On the banks of the lovely St. Croix.

G.W.E. Hill

*Taken from the 1925 *Kabeconian*
(Stillwater High School yearbook)

NOTES